TRANSHUMANISM

A Realistic Future?

Other World Scientific Titles by the Author

Longevity in the 2.0 World: Would Centenarians Become Commonplace?
ISBN: 978-981-120-116-5
ISBN: 978-981-120-203-2 (pbk)

Brain vs Computer: The Challenge of the Century
ISBN: 978-981-3145-54-2
ISBN: 978-981-3145-55-9 (pbk)

Is Man to Survive Science?
ISBN: 978-981-4644-40-2
ISBN: 978-981-4644-41-9 (pbk)

Near Field Optics and Nanoscopy
ISBN: 978-981-02-2349-6

TRANSHUMANISM

A Realistic Future?

Jean-Pierre Fillard

World Scientific

NEW JERSEY · LONDON · SINGAPORE · BEIJING · SHANGHAI · HONG KONG · TAIPEI · CHENNAI · TOKYO

Published by

World Scientific Publishing Co. Pte. Ltd.

5 Toh Tuck Link, Singapore 596224

USA office: 27 Warren Street, Suite 401-402, Hackensack, NJ 07601

UK office: 57 Shelton Street, Covent Garden, London WC2H 9HE

Library of Congress Control Number: 2019052205

British Library Cataloguing-in-Publication Data
A catalogue record for this book is available from the British Library.

TRANSHUMANISM
A Realistic Future?

ISBN 978-981-121-138-6
ISBN 978-981-121-210-9 (pbk)

For any available supplementary material, please visit
https://www.worldscientific.com/worldscibooks/10.1142/11582#t=suppl

Typeset by Stallion Press
Email: enquiries@stallionpress.com

Printed in Singapore

Contents

About Jean-Pierre Fillard

 I came from the University of Algiers when Algeria was a full French territory. I initially specialized in nuclear physics but soon turned to the study of solid state electronics. At that time the "transistor effect" had just been discovered and the buzz was about understanding the electronic mechanisms inside matter. One of the topics was to understand the key issues of the atomic defects lying in the starting semiconductor crystals. This was the field which motivated for me three decades of research.

Now that activity has turned to pure technology, following an endless Moore's law. So I tell people that I was, scientifically, born with the transistor and I died with it! Incidentally, I was elected a fellow of the British Institute of Physics in 1978 and belonged to a flurry of international scientific associations.

In 1967, I obtained a full thesis from the University of Montpellier in France where I was soon upgraded to a full Professor and launched a research laboratory in the field of solid state physics. I am the author or co-author of some 300 publications, communications or collective books and a personal book — *Near Field Optics and Nanoscopy* (World Scientific, 1996). In 1985 I initiated a series of international conferences DRIP (Defect Recognition and Image Processing) which continue around the world every two years.

During these three decades of intense research work, I had the opportunity to visit many places in Europe, the US, Israel, Japan, and even stay in China as invited lecturer. I retired in 1998, as a Professor Emeritus, after winning a cancer episode and I, then, became interested in the evolution and the new prospects opened up by Science and Technology 2.0. This was an opportunity for me to write some books in collaboration with World Scientific and *Transhumanism: A Realistic Future?* is the fourth one.

Introduction

"Transhumanism is an international philosophical movement that advocates for the transformation of the human condition by developing and making widely available sophisticated technologies to greatly enhance human intellect and physiology."[1]

This is the broad definition of transhumanism that can be found on the internet.[2] This "philosophy" especially deals with the benefits (and dangers) we could currently expect from the extrapolation of technologies already available which can deeply change our human nature along with the corresponding environment. Such a thesis is not a new one but one that has resulted from a process of maturation by philosophers. It is not to be confused with science fiction.

From *Gilgamesh* to the *Ubermensch* of Friedrich Nietzsche, a recurrent dream has been access to a different (better) being, and how this can be done. This mainstream thinking converged in the search for ways and means to bring an end to old curses like ageing and death. But are we now facing a philosophical or a science prospect, or both?

Transhumanism can be considered a culmination of continuous evolution from the Big Bang. Darwin theory says that genetic evolution occurs with the millenaries, aimed at making the species more closely adapted to the requirements of the environment. This is the universal rule Nature

---

[1] "A history of transhumanist thought", Nick Boström, *Journal of Evolution and Technology*, February 21, 2006. Available at https://nickbostrom.com/papers/history.pdf
[2] https://en.wikipedia.org/wiki/Transhumanism

(some say God) has arranged. However, taking into account the considerable development of our scientific knowledge, would the theory now have to be reversed by adapting the surrounding to the Trans-human will or even a Post-human one? How soon will such a change come about?

At present, the fantastic take off of knowledge in every domain of Science, stimulated by a powerful technology, triggered the imagination of a realistic possible future well beyond the Darwinian expectations of evolution. Some even evoke the imminent coming of a "Singularity"[3,4] which would bluntly change the existing order of our lives. A dedicated university, the Singularity University, has even been set up in California to develop research and teaching in this field. International meetings have also been held worldwide to coordinate discussions on transhumanism, with the last one in London.[5]

The leading players on the Internet such as GAFAM[6] or NATU in the United States (U.S.),[7] and BATX[8] in China developed practical transhumanist approaches with renewed scientific research axes. In this effort, they have benefitted, for some years, from the vast financial means and huge databases fed by their own social networks.

In that aim two different research trails may be followed: the first one is concerned with biology (brain, genomics, stem cells, and so on) while the second one is "mineral", with computers (software, electronics, robotics, Artificial Intelligence (AI) and the like). Which one will be the first to decisively "improve" Man? No one can yet say but it would take only a good technical trigger to launch the process. Perhaps a mix of both; the computer has begun to know so many things about our body and mental constitution that it might be able to draw pertinent conclusions!

Would the difficult issue of energy be solved for a peaceful future? Since the beginning, new kinds of energy were the trigger for implementa-

---

[3] *The Singularity is Near: When Humans Transcend Biology*, Ray Kurzweil, Penguin Books, 2006.

[4] Singularity, in mathematical language, denotes a sharp rupture in a continuous evolution curve.

[5] TransVision Conference, July 2019.

[6] Google, Amazon, Facebook, Apple, Microsoft.

[7] Netflix, AirBnb, Tesla, Uber.

[8] Baidu, Alibaba, Tencent.

tion of new civilizations: from the discovery of fire to nuclear energy, many ages have succeeded with vapor power, electricity, and others. The 2.0 civilization we have entered could announce the future of transhumanism but no new kind of energy appeared to motivate this change. Robots require energy, not to mention the data centers that run them.

Some have outright suggested[9] the alternative of the creation of an artificial intelligent animal (man or machine, or a mix) which could overcome the native limits of the human species. The natural evolution would then be replaced by an intended transformation. What happens to those who will not be able to follow or reject such collaboration? Would they be considered as a sub-species of sub-humans, like chimpanzees of the future, doomed to disappear because of their worthlessness?

There is no doubt that our global knowledge progresses as never before. Would that mean we can get the power of God to change humanity or create a new one? Human longevity has risen notably to the point where it could be possible to reverse the process of ageing with the possibility of a rejuvenescence that could benefit transhumans. We also imagine being able to create life from scratch. All of this sounds quite crazy but it is so.

Therefore, it can be said that transhumanism is in no way a piece of science fiction to come in a remote future, as the seed has already been sown in our daily life with the occurrence of new behaviors especially attracting the younger generations.

However, this does not come for free, nor does it afford some serious unintended drawbacks. What could be expected in the near future for transhumanism? How would Man be able to collaborate with machines for a better destiny? These questions will be addressed in this book.

Finally, transhumanism takes the form of a pseudo-religion and the question is how compatible this "realistic philosophy" is with established religions. Would these have to mute drastically to adapt to the new transhumanist paradigm or merely disappear under the battering of the technological realities? Some of them are flexible enough not to be appreciably affected, others will require an uneasy adaptation and in some ways a

---

[9]"When will computer hardware match the human brain?", Hans Moravec, *Journal of Evolution and Technology*. Vol. 1, 1998.

defamation of the old rules, but the last ones are rigid enough to already enter into a last chance fight.

The aim of this book is to update readers about the possible future that can be expected from such a projected evolution; after years of dazzling excitement surrounding this topic, time has come for an appeasing discussion.

The book will be structured in three parts:

1. Where does transhumanism come from?
2. What can be expected in the near future?
3. What could be the likely issues to overcome or undergo?

You will note that each part, like the title of the book, includes a question mark at the end.

Part I
Where Does Transhumanism Come From?

Chapter One

The Origins and Further

It was a long, slow process of maturation which prompted us, Nature and man, to our present state. Let me explain how this happened and where our fates have led us, from the prime times of our mortal destinies.

Our current civilization is the outcome of many small elements disorderly accumulated but also several decisive steps that definitively changed our way of life. They resulted in milestones that punctuate our history and irrevocably "changed Man" in his way of life, his behavior, his beliefs thereby affecting his progeny. These changes etched themselves in our habits, irretrievably.

Let us now look at some of these milestones that have brought us unquestionable welfare benefits.

1. From Cro-Magnon to 2.0 World

Undeniably, the first historical step in the evolution of man was the mastering of fire some 450,000 years ago which launched the scientific machine. The progress was clear and present. Then occurred the sedentarization and agriculture appeared after 400,000 years of maturation; after that came the emergence of writing after 8,000 years, followed by the invention of scientific thinking by the Greeks 2,500 years ago. Subsequently also came printing, vapor machines, electricity, nuclear power, and so on. It repeatedly became apparent that the time lapse between each step of progression got shorter and shorter along our human timescale.

This is tentatively sketched in Table 1.1 where are reported the corresponding evolutions of the mean life expectation and the world population. The trigger for each of the new steps in civilizations was the successive discoveries of a new kind of available energy which brought about a new level of comfort and security. However, if the previous civilizations were all preceded and induced by a new form of energy, this is no longer true today where the digital age 2.0 did not arise from a new energy form but from a scientific discovery that upset everything: the transistor effect, giving rise to our current digital world. Could this indicate that we have entered for the first time a new way of doing?

Along this extended path, well before the established transhumanists arrived, the idea of improving our being has long been addressed. The great epic of *Gilgamesh* may be the first historical evocation of a "Superman" (a dream obviously inspired by the Gods) who benefited from an extension of the mean human status. Then there were numerous searches for a recipe to reach immortality: the fountain of youth, the elixir of long life, and any kinds of effort to prevent ageing and death but nothing worked.

The transhumanist philosophy found its roots in the French Renaissance (15th century) with the philosophy of the Enlightenment[1] when Pic de la Mirandole invited Man "to sculpt his own statue". Later Marquis de Condorcet and Benjamin Franklin were speculating about a possible application of the (young) medical science to the extension of human life. Finally Darwin said that "it becomes probable that Humanity, as we know it now, would not still reached its final state of evolution but more likely a phase of beginning".[2]

Julian Huxley[3] (a brother of Aldous) was the first to use the word "Transhuman" (in 1957) to describe "a man who remains a man but transcends

---

[1] *Discours de la dignité de l'homme*, Pic de la Mirandole — 1486, Trad. Yves Hersant, Paris, 1993.

[2] "A history of transhumanist thought", Nick Boström, *Journal of Evolution and Technology*, 14(1), 1–25, 2005.

[3] "Transhumanism", Julian Huxley, 1957. See: http://sniadecki.wordpress.com/2015/01/21/ huxley-transhumanisme/ (in French)

Table 1.1. Schematic evolution map of humanity.

			Longevity	Estimated World Population
Digital age		AI mastered Energy	90	7,5 B
Nuclear age		Nuclear Energy	65	3 B
Electricity age		Electrical Energy	45	1,5 B
Steam machine		Vapour Energy	35	1 B
Bronze Iron civilisation Coal age		Control of fire Energy	30 ?	4 M
Making fire Wood age		Discovery of Energy	< 30	10 K

himself by deploying new possibles to and for his human nature". In his mind that means to improve the performance of individuals through eugenics.

The current meaning of the word originated in 1980 when American futurologists began to give a structure to the transhumanist movement. They emphasized hybridized humans that would be given such capacities as to be qualified as posthumans.[2]

Finally the current definition of transhumanism was given by Max More[4] as follows:

- Human condition promotion through technologies for life improvement aimed at eliminating ageing, enhancing intellectual, physical, or psychological abilities.
- A study of the benefits, dangers, and ethics induced by the development and implementation of these above techniques.

The transhumanist prospect of changing humanity raised enthusiasm as well as concerns from various origins. Francis Fukuyama[5] (a political scientist at John Hopkins University) was one of the main detractors, explaining in detail that this idea was one of the most dangerous. In actual fact, we have already entered the transhumanist age without realizing it, and so we, then, have to put up with it.

It is also worth mentioning that, together with the foreseen changes biology may induce in human nature, there is also an issue with the relations of man with machines[6] which influence increases unstoppingly. Artificial Intelligence has become a strong competitor challenging the human one previously considered as definitely superior. This field is a major one in the transhumanist philosophy.

We shall later develop this important field but let us have some words as an introduction to this domain. When the computer was born (in the eighties) it soon crossed the minds of specialists that it could (one day to come) become a serious challenger of the brain in the two main branches of basic human activity: logic (algorithms) and memory (data). This gave rise to a new specialty very widely appreciated by the proponents of transhumanism: the development of an AI that could be as well initiated starting from an exact copy (hum?!) of the human brain (supposing there could be a convenient model of it) or a free extrapolation in a model which has, yet, to be invented from scratch.

---

[4] http://humanityplus.org/philosophy/transhumanist-faq/
[5] *Our Posthuman Future: Consequence of the Biotechnology Revolution*, Francis Fukuyama, Farrar, Strauss & Giroux, New York, 2002.
[6] "When will computer hardware match the human brain?", Hans Moravec, *Journal of Evolution and Technology*," Vol. 1, 1998.

At the moment we can say that recorded data are accumulating in huge centers all around the world whereas algorithms are improving through Deep Learning to dig into this incredible mass of information. That is, for now, enough to encourage the wildest dreams of people concerned with our possible future.

The first transhumanists used to meet together in the early eighties in the University of California Los Angeles, which became the main active center of this futuristic ideology thus giving rise to many dedicated conferences. In 1998 Nick Boström and David Pearce founded the World Transhumanist Association (WTA), a non-governmental organization active at the international level to promote transhumanism in the scientific community and to public authorities.

On this special occasion the question of equitable access to the techniques of human improvement for people coming from different social classes or different nationalities was asked.[7] A pessimistic point of view was developed by Kevin Warwick who said, "There will be implanted or hybrid people and they will dominate the world. The others, who were not, will not be more useful than the current cows in the field... Those who will decide to remain human and refuse any 'improvement' will have a big handicap. They would constitute a subspecies and be the chimpanzee of the future."

Of course this is a very schematic cartoony view. Even if it becomes feasible to make "intelligence improved men" that does not mean they will be powerful at the same time. There are currently many intelligent men (or women!) in established societies, but who cares? What power do they have to change the world?

In 2008, WTA changed its name to "Humanity+" and published a magazine to present news and ideas on the transhumanist philosophy.[8]

1.1. *Modern times are coming*

Today, the gurus of the future are back with forecasting theories which were discrete before. It was not until 1970 that the book *Future Shock* by

---

[7] "Humanity, the remix", Alyssa Ford, *Utne*, May, June 2005.
[8] http://hplusmagazine.com/

Alvin Toeffler became a worldwide bestseller[9] and has sold over 6 million copies. With some 50 years of hindsight, one uncovers previsions that had been deadlocks; some were successful but, as a matter of fact we did not yet discover the current avenues which have escaped predictions but finally came out on top.

These gurus do not belong to any kinds of sect. They aim at teaching pragmatic working methods and propose new perspectives to economic or industrial executives of all disciplines in order to anticipate future opportunities of the world economy since *business is business*!

The stage preceding the avalanche of discoveries was the transistor, only 60 years ago. The electron was tamed using a specific technology that will allow it to perform marvels of acrobatics which will shake our lives. The computer will become part of our activities with the Internet and many other implications which have a direct impact on our behavior.

This revolution was triggered by three "inconspicuous" researchers at Bell Labs: William Shockley, John Bardeen, and Walter Brattain in 1947. Never did they imagine for a second then that they would that soon upset the world but they did. However, they never received the public fame they deserved even though they were awarded the prestigious Nobel Prize in 1956. Their discovery of the "transistor effect" was too technical to be appreciated by the average citizen.

After the initial highlight of this experimental breakthrough it took some ten years of maturation and technical developments to obtain the first operational transistor and turn it into a real industrial product. The original components were the size of a moth equipped with three electrical wires. That was rather rough but worked confidently enough to give rise immediately to applications. This subject shall be considered again later in detail.

The first radio receiver[10] fully equipped with these solid state components was commercially available in 1954. At that time, the transistor was made of a little bar taken out of a Germanium crystal and equipped with three electrodes. This was quite cumbersome (compared to the current

---

[9] *Future Shock*, Alvin Toeffler, Bantam Book, 1970.

[10] "Regency TR-1" produced by Texas Instruments (Dallas) and Industrial Development Engineering Associates (Indianapolis).

components) but performed well enough to profitably replace the previous calorific vacuum tubes. Then the technical evolution was dazzling; Silicon took over from Germanium, giving rise to the Field Effect Transistor (FET) and current Integrated Circuits (IC) entering the micro-scale domain.

All of that goes with the ever-increasing performance of electronic instruments: all-purpose computers, digital imaging, any kind of displays, sensors, intelligent robots, near field microscopes, etc. New instruments make it possible to build up new components which generate new instruments and the loop gets closed, endlessly.

A very astute engineer at Intel understood that it was possible to extend the technology to a versatile, polyvalent, light, and easily movable computer. Intel refused the project and the engineer came to Paris to build the first dinosaur of the PC[11] family called "Micral I".[12] Programming took place directly, electrically, with switches bit after bit! Heroic but so historical! But evolution laws immediately seized the opportunity and applied towards an endless better adaptation. A real demand existed for such a small unit; the idea of the home PC merged and successive more and more adapted and sophisticated versions were to appear under various brands and other names. Not even the boldest forecaster (the most futuristic transhumanist!) would have imagined, some 40 years ago, such an impressive mutation that the universe imposed on us and which we willingly accepted. Nobody could have suspected that within so short a while the PC, a machine, would become a so friendly (?) daily fellow, witness of our intimate life.

So Darwin's software won! But what could we expect now for the next forty years ahead with such incredible nanotechnologies, with electronic components so intelligent and minuscule? Would it be unconceivable to directly connect our brains with this machine so that it would no longer be qualified as inanimate and the capacities of which gradually increase? All of that is food for transhumanism perspectives.

---

[11] Personal Computer.

[12] With this Micral we were able, with Dr Michel Castagné, to perform the first computer driven laboratory experiences.

Man applauds the coming of scientific progresses; is that for his own interest or for reaching an ultimate step of the Darwinian evolution of the species? What is plain is that seismic shifts (for good or ill) should inevitably come in a not-so- remote future. Whether we like it or not, they are coming and we shall accept them. So how far may transhumanists be involved in that forecasting?

Nevertheless, the Grand Chief Guru of forward thinking, Ray Kurzweil[13] (economist, philosopher, software specialist, businessman, and so on) foresees a near "Singularity" to come. This word is defined in mathematical language as "a sharp and irreversible rupture in a continuous process". This singularity would correspond to a sudden mutation in our ways of life and of our deep being, to come in the middle of this century. This could be considered as a rather schematic view; it would be more likely that a series of singularities would come, each coming from a decisive and specialized breakthrough.

Now let us come back to Cro-Magnon discovering the benefits of fire in a cave. Such an improvement in his living standards was the first diversion from the pure biological program initially provided by Nature for animals. As a consequence, the life expectation began to slightly extend and this was a real bonus for the time delay dedicated to reproduction. Hopefully Man benefits from a rather extensive period for reproduction. So the population was able to grow and counteracted for the first time the natural laws by, then, adapting the environment to the species.

During these rough primitive times child mortality was severe and selection was merciless. This was a natural pledge for a favored genomic evolution toward the more adapted species. So the reproduction rhythm had to be especially fast in order to energetically "shuffle the cards".

Today, the healthcare available for babies has inhibited such a genomic filter. Deviations can freely propagate albeit the more severe ones can be prevented by a careful early detection. This is a way to reconcile with the prescriptions of Nature. Nevertheless the "genetical

---

[13] Some do not hesitate to call him a "high level charlatan". However he has been hired by Google to head the Department of Research and Evaluation which assesses projects of the future. That is certainly not for nothing.

filter" does not work as initially intended, so generating in the long run a "pollution" of our global genetic heritage. Hopefully such a drift is very slow.

1.2. *The time for biology*

Time has come for Man to directly interfere with this natural organization. The mystery of heredity was discovered by James Watson and Francis Crick in 1953 to be located in an interminable molecule named DNA. They initially thought that at least a century would be necessary to keep clear of this complexity but, nevertheless, 10 years were enough for Craig Venter to be able to decrypt this structure.

A multitude of scientists jumped in to analyze the properties of this fundamental biological element and quite soon the new technique of "CRISPR[14] cas 9" recently opened new horizons in this field and allowed man to freely change a sequence. The new science of epigenetics was born. That was an opened door for transhumanists to imagine a new kind of humanity that would be adapted to any requirement by optimizing the DNA molecules. From now on, excitement is at the zenith with this opened access to all sorts of manipulation, from extended longevity to the improved, augmented, transformed man, or the artificial[15] "designer baby" (zero defect ensured) grown out of utero.

The old dream of Pygmalion who felt in love with its statue Galatea has become reality. This is fantastic but also incredibly frightening. Now that biologists can play with DNA, they struggle in vain (to date!) to find a gene directly related to death. Short of reaching this Holy Grail, they found that many indirect contributions arise in the mechanism of ageing and are trying to stop or even reverse the process. The unsubstantiated theories of the transhumanists find here a very strong support for their predications.

---

[14] Contrary to popular belief CRISPR was not born in Bethlehem but in Berkeley in 2012 from the work of Emmanuelle Charpentier and Jennifer Doudna.

[15] First trials were already undertaken, the first time on sheep, but more recently a couple of twin sisters were born in China using genetically modified gametes to prevent any risk of being contaminated by the HIV virus. This is a very first step.

George Church (who is in no way an entertainer) even talks about obtaining a possible "ageing reversal" or "rejuvenation" process which could drastically change the equation and boost the process of evolution. He said: "there are a fair number of precedents for this in animals but the idea is to get it transferred to humans", and, on top of that, this genetical rectification should be transmitted to man's descendants! This would certainly bring a "necessity" to live which could drastically temper the previous effects of "chance" of death.

2. What about God and Nature?

In the remote epochs of life, the unit of time was a million years; this allowed for dinosaurs to evolve quietly. Darwin said it was a slow biomechanical process of selection/evolution driven by chance and necessity. This was intended to be a perfectly deterministic mechanism driven by error/success logic. God (Nature) launched the machine and let it go, for better or worse.

How to deal with machines we are expected to live with? Most transhumanists do not trust a transcendent soul. They more likely trust in a compatibility (to find) of the human mind with the digital hardware; they guess that, at some (utopian) point, human consciousness could be transferred into a dedicated media, possibly even in a simulated reality. Tipler[16] imagined that such an achievement in a mega computer might take the dimension of a "post-human God". Such a bold extrapolation was actively fought by a large panel of scientists and philosophers like Hans Moravec or Marvin Minsky.

2.1. The necessity of religions

Tribes of these remote times needed a necessary cohesion to survive and defend them. That has generated the mythical requirement of a common belief (and associated rules to be observed) that was to become entrenched. This psychological training was an essential contribution to the sense of collective belonging and has been a psychological haven.

---

[16] *The Physics of Immortality: Modern Cosmology, God and the Resurrection of the Dead*, Frank G Tipler, New York: Double Day, 1994.

Most famous civilizations (the Pharaohs, Greeks and Romans, even the Incas) benefitted from a strict regulation by their own religion. These civilizations left significant archaeological remains and cultural relics that survived until present day. Each of these previous religions arose from a lack of ascertained knowledge about our external world. The religion of the Greeks has been elaborated from the folk traditions of *The Iliad* and *Odysseus*. Every people agreed and adapted to the exigencies ... or are invited to drink the hemlock as Socrates did. Nevertheless it appeared as evidence, in the long run, that there was no Zeus atop Mount Olympus and so the Greek religion vanished.

These religions have deeply assisted but never motivated any civilization (but rather wars). The ancient religions had to disappear to make room for the current ones (and their derivatives). This is pure Darwinism. Would, now, transhumanism be part of the religions of the future?

The fears that dominated in these remote times (cold, heat, hunger, wild beasts (and humans), health, and death) have been replaced by others, equally oppressive (cancer, nuclear, pollution, viruses, pesticides, and so forth) but death still remains even as life expectancy rockets. This can still be considered a divine decision despite our best efforts to prevent (or at least delay) it.

Science and Technology have begun offering perspectives that have up to now been inconceivable. That has called into question the belief in any religion and any God. Would that shock wave be strong enough to shake the very basis of religions? Would the idea of God be so essential to our lives? Would this idea also have to change and adapt for survival? Each one will react as he may but would a collective movement be generated? As a provisional answer Ray Kurzweil says: "If I was asked if God exists ... I would answer, not yet" and he dared to tell Bill Gates that "If Matter and Energy were saturated with intelligence, 'it'[17] will wake up, be conscious and outstandingly intelligent".

Dinosaurs have disappeared (unless we could clone a new one!). Now, the time scale has shrunk drastically down to a year unit and changes are initiated by human intellectual procedures that are less deterministic and foreseeable than the geological ones. We are on the verge of changing our

---

[17] That makes reference to a "charismatic operating system" !

own biological nature. Is God (Nature) to still let it go and not care? Some have said that believing in God changes the brain. By extension, would this mean that if God is to be rubbed out of our minds this would cause us to revert to a previous state? As Voltaire put it, "Man invented God, not the opposite".

It is worth noting that any new religion to emerge since Islam[18] did so some millennium and a half ago. Does this mean that our inventiveness concerning the idea of God is less and less essential and we have to be satisfied with the present beliefs? To be convinced now people would require more compelling arguments and stronger evidence than in the Middle Ages (although people always deeply need to be comforted).

Religions are silent (all of them). We have entered a new knowledge age which brings us sophisticated opportunities to challenge still more the natural order and, inexorably, changes will come. Is there a destiny behind? Would we have to get through a "Singularity" as transhumanists suggest?

For some time attempts were developed to explain religious experience and behavior in neuroscientific terms and correlate neural phenomena with experiences of spirituality. Aldous Huxley was the first to use the term of *neurotheology* which was intended to refer to a pseudo-science devoted to a "cognitive neuroscience" of religious experience and spirituality in a scientific or philosophical context. This was quite unclear until Laurence McKinney published the first book[19] on the subject in 1994.

According to McKinney's theory, pre-frontal development, in humans, creates an illusion of chronological time as a fundamental part of normal adult cognition past the age of three. The inability of the adult brain to retrieve earlier images experienced by an infantile brain creates questions such as "Where did I come from?" and "Where does it all go?", which McKinney suggests led to the creation of various religious explanations. This leads to a reinterpretation of religion based on current neuroscientific research. Some scientists working in the field hypothesize that the basis of spiritual experience arises in neurological physiology.

---

[18] Only sects were proposed, but they have not gathered enough traction for purpose of discussion.

[19] *Neurotheology: Virtual Religion in the 21st Century*, Laurence O McKinney, The American Institute for Mindfulness, 1994.

All of these efforts still remain quite messy in spite of many experimental attempts to evidence a neurophysiological effect by magnetic stimulation, fMRI neuroimaging or psychoactive ingredients. However, this evidently contributes to the field of transhumanism.

2.2. Present status

A large majority of transhumanists do not trust in the possibility of a personal dedicated soul, they are secular or atheist. They do not imagine a possible transcendence but admit a feasible compatibility of spirit with machines that would allow downloading a spirit into a computer. In such an eventuality it must be supposed that the machine will be in a permanent continuous relation with the brain in order to upload in real time every change occurring in the mind (it is well known that "spirit is ready"). So what might happen after death? Would the machine continue autonomously?

Some say that transhumanism is a materialist pseudo-religion centered on brain behavior. Futurists speculate about the next few years and imagine that current works in the field might lead to radical developments allowing deep improvements to the human. Possibly, a post-Darwinian phase of our existence where random genetical mutation might be replaced by voluntary changes guided by reason, morals, or simply ethical purposes.

Google has become one of the major sponsors for the transhumanist movement with the support of NBIC[20] industries and the active collaboration of Ray Kurzweil. The "Calico" department especially deals with the fight against ageing and associated diseases. As a matter of fact there is also strong opposition to these views. The objections relate to the basic principles of morals and pragmatism. The "Center for Genetics" was created in 2001 to counteract the transhumanist's projects and especially human cloning. The Vatican has also expressed a clear opposition whereas Teilhard de Chardin expressed a possible compatibility with Catholicism in exchange for some evolution in the current dogma.

Man had taken a long time to become "Homo sapiens"; now that he trusts to master everything,[21] would he, all a sudden, turn to a "Homo

---

[20] Nanotechnologies, Biotechnologies, Information, Cognitive Sciences.

[21] *Homo Deus*, Yuval Noah Harari, Harwill Secker, London, 2015.

Deus"? Transhumanists are not alone in dealing with these issues. Teilhard de Chardin was fascinated by the emerging technologies of the computers and foresaw that they could lead us to a new stage of consciousness. He said, in 1950, in his premonitory essay,[22] that an "ultra-humanity" was coming and "that without deep changes, religion is to fade away in the night". The incredible grip of religions on the minds of men will become less and less effective due to extensive information.

Transhumanism is well aware of these issues, namely the relationship between religion and present scientific requirements. Even Christopher Benek[23] proclaimed himself a transhumanist pastor to promote a common bond between faith and technology. He says (take a deep breath): "In my opinion, the word "artificial" is a misleading and a somewhat unhelpful term. It implies that humanity is the only form of intelligence. We know this is not the case. But my short answer, if we are talking about autonomous, strong AI, is yes … because from a theological perspective, we are God's AI."

Now would AI artifacts improve man's intelligence as machines empowered his strength? Serguei Brin (from Google X Lab) foresees: "we will make machines that can reason, think and do things better than we can" whereas the Israelian mathematician Doron Zeilberger adds that "the logic of the computer is to surpass our conceptual understanding". That's a lot! As a matter of fact the Delph temple carved inscription "Man, know thyself and you will know the Universe and the Gods" is more than ever on the agenda.

The question of God versus machine was at the origin of a stream of unfounded and unfinished discussions until now. Ray Kurzweil[24] discussed this profoundly without reaching any firm conclusion. Would neurons be pure machines or is their organization more subtle? Dembski[25] agrees that they need "extra material factors" whereas Jay Richards[26] asks

---

[22] *La place de l'Homme dans la Nature*, Pierre Teilhard de Chardin, Albin Michel, Paris, 1956.

[23] https://www.psychologytoday.com/blog/the-digital-self/201705/the-pastor-who-found-god-in-technology

[24] Kurzweil, *Singularity*, p. 477.

[25] *The Design Inference: Eliminating Chance Through Small Probabilities*, William Dembski, Cambridge University Press, 2002.

[26] *Are We Spiritual Machines?: Ray Kurzweil vs. the Critics of Strong A.I.*, George F. Filder, Ray Kurzweil, and Jay W. Richards, Discovery Institute, 2001.

"are we spiritual machines?". Kurzweil answers: "So, evolution moves inexorably toward our conception of God, albeit never reaching this ideal". Then God is unable to manifest Himself in a machine because the machine has not the necessary transcendence. All of that was proposed 16 years ago, is it still so convincing? Not so sure!

3. Darwin and Evolution

The brain is on the way to be deciphered and, possibly, copied; we have entered a pure Eugenics domain; what does remain for God? We do know that the mind is fragile but things change if it is to be replaced by a purely rational and autonomous machine which does not doubt and begins to think. The machine is in no way afraid of death, neither of pain nor any danger (except if it has been taught to). Would everything be a matter of logic? Would it be mandatory to teach the machine a dose of fear, a dose of morals, somewhat similar to the robot's limitations and warnings previously requested by Alan Turing?

3.1. *Is transhumanism an evolution in itself?*

The transhumanist movement did not come from nothing; from the earliest epochs, Man dreamed of a better destiny without waiting for an after death Paradise; a destiny of extended life and a control of his own being. This idea can be found among philosophers for a while; perhaps Lamarck paved the way and Darwin followed with the theory of "transformism" and evolution which were further considered as natural laws. This was then refined and supported with the discovery of genetics by Gregor Mendel[27] which is now widely accepted. Then Monod commented: "what is true for the bacteria is equally true for the elephant".

They all agree that evolution does not aim at an ultimate perfection (human being) but at a better adaptation to the environment in order to simply survive. The only limit is to provide time enough for the species to reproduce. The individual does not matter from a biological point of view, the only purpose being the continuity of the species.

---

[27] *Versuche über Pflanzenhybriden*, Grégor Mendel, Verhandlun-gen des naturforschenden Vereines, Brunn, 1866.

From that on, some visionaries as Steve Jobs said "we cannot predict the future except if we are able to make it". This is an open door to science and technology which frightened some pessimists like Thomas Robert Malthus who foresaw an inescapable global starvation due to the shortage of resources the planet could provide us.

3.2. *Rejuvenescence to counter Darwin*

From time immemorial, people on all continents were asking this essential question "what means eternity and how to reach it?". In ancient Egypt this issue was a real obsession which led Pharaohs to build monuments robust enough to defy millennia and bear witness of their being and their beliefs, failing themselves to biologically survive over such an endless period. In the same vein is the cult of the mummies which are, maybe, waiting for a possible cloning?

Biology is now on the verge of giving out the last secrets of the mechanisms of life to overcome the ageing process and, why not, master the fate of death. Two contributions were proposed to explain the cellular degradation: one comes from a deregulation in the mutations, the other from "accidental damages". The former explanation relies on the fact that at the cellular level, mutations can be accompanied by alterations in the protein function and regulation. These perturbed mutations are then replicated when the cell replicates. All contributions agree with the idea that mutation, as distinct from DNA damage, could be the primary cause of ageing; but that idea has failed to gain significant experimental support: in mice, for instance, there is no increase in mutations in the brain with ageing.

It then follows that the main contribution in the ageing process would come from damages as a consequence of unrepaired accumulation of naturally occurring DNA damage; "damage" in this context is a DNA alteration that has an abnormal structure. These damages can contribute to ageing either indirectly (by increasing the apoptosis phenomenon which is a kind of cellular suicide or spontaneous cellular senescence) or directly (by increasing an internal cell dysfunction).

Among the most important organs that can be affected by cellular ageing these are the brain and the muscles (the heart). Then extended longevity represents a continuous fight against the laws of nature which are not programmed for that. The critical issue remains that we can live longer but in good health and shape, mentally as well as physically.

So scientists are now looking to reverse the cerebral death, to reverse the ageing process and, once again that works with mice! They already found (in the mouse[28] alas) the primary factor that is called GDF11; fortunately it could be transposable to humans. This is still very prospective but encouraging results were already reached. Ageing is a very plastic process especially in humans. These results were obtained by researchers at the Salk Institute in California where the animals were turned younger and lived 30% longer. That is a very good start! So, please, hurry up!

Meanwhile it was also found that stimulating four genes (Yamanaka factor) turns the clock back on the human skin cells (*in vitro*). Would that lead to nurture sound hopes of getting younger as well as older at the same time? A direct challenge with Nature is so open!

Fabulous experimental perspectives have risen to master what some are calling[29] "rejuvenescence" or "rejuvenation" or "ageing reversal" that is to say, purely and simply, the reversal of the ageing process by addressing cellular fouling and controlling the destructive proteins.

4. Origins of the Transhumanist Philosophy

4.1. *Intentions and perspectives*

Transhumanism is a kind of "think tank", at an international level, bringing together an extended variety of people such as: philosophers, biologists, neurologists, roboticists, computer scientists, AI developers, and every sort of cognitivist! They all aim at deciphering the influence of current scientific discoveries upon future ways of life that could appear soon. Each one his own model and his own convictions!

Many transhumanists consider that science and technology would be able to counteract disease, disability, even poverty at a large collective

---

[28] Intrinsically, there is no direct interest to make mice immortal but each one will add what they please.

[29] "If you don't die, you can't reach God", Rejuvenaction. Available at: https://rejuvenaction.wordpress.com/answers-to-objections/objections-to-living-forever/if-you-dont-die-you-cant-reach-god/

scale and could bring up innovative social systems; these philosophers emphasize a humanity where the natural evolution be replaced by a deliberate transformation. The main interest, however, relies on the accessible improvements of the human body at an individual scale.

The term "transhumanism" (or H+) is frequently used as a synonym of "human improvements" such as ageing control or even ageing reversal through biological ways or bluntly digital substitution. Think-tanks such as Neohumanitas in Switzerland promote reflection and discussion on the possible socio-ethical consequences of the development of bio-technologies for humans.

4.2. Technical approach

Whereas many transhumanists have an abstract and theoretical approach, some others have proposed precise changes of the human body, including hereditary ones. They are mainly concerned with the methods dedicated to the improvement of the nervous system (memory and some other potentialities) through a modification of the peripheral nervous system or simply through an artificial exo-cortex. The brain is considered by the transhumanists as the basic thread to the personality and hence it is the main goal of their aspirations.

All of that procedure is aimed at improving man by bringing him "wisdom" through a better knowledge of oneself and of nature. The perfection of reasoning would have to result in an explanation of the world even if some are still intuitively defending the possibility of virtual worlds beyond our understanding. The "nonexistence" of things always was the focus of bitter discussions.

Consciousness in itself remains a deep individual mystery close to existential beliefs and religions; many research programs all over the world are devoted to and mixing many different disciplines.

4.3. Playing God? A leap forward to what?

The transhumanists strongly support NBIC technologies also with futuristic sciences like Simulated Reality, strong AI, brain investigations, and so on. They hope[30] that these techniques of human improvement will facilitate more decisive improvements for the 21st century humanity and also apply to the Man/Machine interface as well as applications to the soldier conditioning. There is a debate, close to science fiction, about a possible alteration of the brain to induce decisive advantages[31] for "super soldiers" on the battlefield.

All of this converges toward techniques which will be able to promote the creation of new human capacities even if they imply, at the limit, the outright replacement (in a post-humanist view) of the human species by a new paradigm: the Cyborg. We are very close to the domain of God!

"This is an attempt to reevaluate the full definition of the human being as we generally conceive it … this is a constructive and long term approach of our new situation" said the philosopher Nick Boström.

These transhumanists finally emphasize a "post-Darwinian" phase of the human existence in which the changes will become guided by reason, morals, or an ethics beyond the usual biological limitations.

Obviously all of these positions lead to numerous controversies.[32] One direction of them is a pragmatic criticism of the objectives. Another is a moral criticism of the principles. L Alexandre, for instance, said: "a new religious paradigm has surfaced: this is no longer the renouncement of the atheist being alone in the Universe but henceforth the proud assertion that Man is now able to do anything, included creating the living and even reestablish himself."

Others foresee the possibility of "eugenic wars" with the return of genetical discrimination in direct human rights abuses and the genocide of races considered as lower classes;[33] a kind of society made of "cyborgs+" and "minus". In that domain some as Phillipe de Villiers[34] consider that

---

[30] *Converging Technologies for Improving Human Performance*, Mihail C. Roco and William Sims Bainbridge, eds., Springer, 2004.

[31] *Mind Wars: Brain Research and National Defense*, Jonathan D Moreno, Dana Press, 2006.

[32] *Radical Evolution: The Promise and Peril of Enhancing Our Minds, Our Bodies — And What It Means to be Human*, Joel Garreau, Broadway, 2006.

[33] War Against the Weak, Edwin Black, Four Walls Eight Windows, 2003.

[34] *Le Moment Est Venu de Dire ce que J'ai vu*, Phillipe de Villiers, Albin Michel, 2015.

"there will be no more place for disables, weak-kneed or faint-hearted, not any place for the "sub-humans".

As matter of fact, from the very beginning when Men discovered how to make fire, he has never ceased defying the laws of Nature (i.e. God for many people) and transhumanism strongly favors such an attitude.

Chapter Two

The Theories

With the coming of the 19th century, the idea arose[1] that Man could favorably evolve under the influence of a modern civilization inspired by science, the model of achievement being obviously the occidental civilization; this gave rise to the Eugenist theories which aim at promoting technics to improve the genetic patrimony and achieve "perfect babies" or at least newborns free from serious illnesses. Today Science provides us with a huge amount of knowledge in all areas to the point that it becomes realistic that, in a near future, the basic constitution of our body could be repaired, improved or even "augmented". All of that contributes to the transhumanism philosophy with the wish to extend our life beyond the current standards.

Beyond these futuristic biological forecasting, transhumanism also deals with the implication of machines in our constitution, directly with dedicated electronic circuits or indirectly by adapting our environment (communications, data management, instruments, and so on). Progress remains unstoppable; it works regardless of what we oppose; awe as well as wonderment take turns to appear in global opinions and they impact or even promote futures technologies. There is no possible relinquishment to this move. We cannot get rid of the "bad" part of the technology and retain only the "good" part. Benefits and risks are deeply entangled.

---

[1] *Francis Galton: The Life and Work of a Victorian Genius*, Derek W Forrest, Taplinger Pub Co, 1974.

Aero-Cab Station

Figure 2.1.   A vision of the 2.0 era as imagined in 1900.

Transhumanists are the forecasters of our times. With due respect to Science, they are in somewhat the same position as their previous colleagues of the 1900 years. Figure 2.1 is an example of their vision of the year 2000 society! People at that time imagined that the rising Science would bring them to quite a different world where unthinkable things will be commonplace. A century after we are still waiting for the "aero-cars" the Pythonesses have promised, but so many other unforeseen things have emerged since then, which could have hardly been imagined before!

1. Underlying Theories of Transhumanism

Transhumanism "philosophy" is the result of a long lying series of ways of thinking drawn for centuries, essentially motivated by a quest for immortality and, more generally hosted in the "humanism" movement of the 19th century. Many thinkers have contributed from Pic de la Mirandole, Marquis de Condorcet, Benjamin Franklin, Friedrich Nietzsche, Charles Darwin, Aldous Huxley, and many others, each one with his own vision of a possible future assisted by science. They all are convinced that we have not yet reached a definitive position in the evolution of the human being, and that something new is to be expected sooner or later.

The very real break toward the modern views came in the early sixties with Marvin Minsky[2] when a debate surged between the human intelligence and an artificial one which just became conceivable. He was soon followed by Hans Moravec[3] and Raymond Kurzweil[4] and in 1998 the philosophers Nick Boström and David Pearce founded the World Transhumanist Association (WTA) to promote the anti-ageing techniques and related ethical problems. They were especially concerned by the social issues which could be a potential impediment to their futuristic projects.

1.1. Transhumanism or posthumanism

There is a debate about the concept of transhumanism with respect to that of posthumanism. Are they necessarily intimately related? Something both these philosophers share is the common vision of new intelligent species to emerge as a "natural" evolution of humanity. Subtle discussions seek to clarify which one is the result of the other. Critics of transhumanism[5] (Christians, Conservatives, or Progressives) say it is nothing else than a preliminary version of a definitive posthumanism which is to settle down indefinitely.

Transhumanism highlights the evolutionist aspect of the human being that will soon lead to a cognitive improvement to a posthuman[6] artificial future. Some humanists think that transhumanists make the difference because they are mostly involved in the technical implications of human

---

[2] "Steps toward artificial intelligence", Marvin Minsky, *Proceedings of the IRE*, January 1960. Available at: https://courses.csail.mit.edu/6.803/pdf/steps.pdf

[3] "When will computer hardware match the human brain?", Hans Moravec, *Journal of Evolution and Technology*, Vol. 1, 1998.

[4] The Age of Spiritual Machines, Ray Kurzweil, Viking Adult, 1999.

[5] "Transhumanism and Posthumanism", in *Encyclopedia of Bioethics*, Christopher Hooks and Stephen G Post, Macmillan, 2004.

[6] *Citizen Cyborg: Why Democratic Societies Must Respond to the Redesigned Human of the Future*, James Hughes, Westview Press, 2004.

issues, especially the relation to death. So they turn away from the social aspect and the pure philosophical spirit of humanism.[7]

Nevertheless, many transhumanists contribute to a search for social innovations by eliminating the congenital barriers of the physical as well as the psychological into an ideal of a uniform (?) equality. They hope that it would become possible for the humans to take control of their evolution; the natural evolution would then be substituted by a deliberate change. Such a perspective might be potentially detrimental to the preservation of the human health if the new technics to come are not satisfactorily mastered. So opponents to transhumanism often refer to the social movement of the Luddists in the 19th century which was opposed to the replacement of human workers by machines.

Be that at it may, the continuous push toward new technical landscapes certainly implies that deep social changes will result. Not to give in to the doomsday predictions of mass starvation or lack of food for an excessively large population (Malthus), the "progresses" in robotization anyway already nurture some anxiety about the sustainability of some traditional jobs. The solution to this issue lie in a permanent recycling of the concerned people; the professions which could escape this destiny remain rather scarce except, maybe the hairdressers! We cannot imagine a robot doing that job! Or maybe the post-humans (men and women) would need a biological change in order to be bald! A touch of humor is required in such a sad perspective!

To introduce a distinction between "trans" and "post" humanism is rather subtle. Some say that "trans" refers to an intermediate phase where the body's limits would evolve toward new limits whereas "post" refers to new entities the body limits of which would be drastically augmented. All of these conceptions vary with the context concerned and with the authors. Following the philosopher David Doat and the historian Franck Darmour:[8] "they are cultural ways of thinking that clearly are positioned aside the modern humanism in order to propose different suites".

---

[7] *The Future of Human Nature*, Langdon Wienner, Harold Bailie, and Timothy Casey, MIT Press

[8] *Transhumanisme: quell avenir pour l'humanité*, Franck Darmour and David Doat, Le Cavalier Bleu, 2018.

In such a way the post-human would be a human technologically transformed into a different "being" which possibly would have no need to biologically be "born" (as usually intended) and consequently also not need to die.[9] With the future post-humanism Man will self-produce. So the post-human will[10] "live in a post-reality where he (it?) will negotiate his post-relations and his post-psychism with subtlety".

So, as long as transhumanism implicitly only aims at being a quasi-religion, posthumanism aims at surpassing the human potential currently limited. These two perspectives could be considered as fundamentally distinct and successive. As Kevin Kelly has said about transhumanism: "Yet its claims are so outrageous that if true, it would mean... well ...the end of the world as we know it, and the beginning of utopia".

As stated by Max More: we do not need another dogma or cult; "Singularitarianism" is not a system of beliefs or unified viewpoints, it is an insight that causes one to rethink everything from the nature of health and wealth to the nature of death itself.

1.2. The accelerating technology

The ongoing acceleration of technology arises from the progress of available products, mainly the performance of integrated circuits which allow faster computations and larger memories.

In this way the most impressive field is Artificial Intelligence: a domain in which transhumanists are deeply involved in, even if many of them are not sufficiently technically qualified to comment. If men, one day to come, are to be taken over by machines then it will certainly be the pure result of a dominant AI. The issue is serious but the brain is flexible and the human intelligence a very complex and not yet assessed organization.

The success of human evolution also relies on the diversity of minds, each one being more skillful in a domain than the other in a different one. Biological evolution is not a matter of a single narrow species but of a variety of them. This results in a diversified accumulation of distributed knowledges

---

[9] *How the Mind Works*, Steven Pinker, Norton, 1997.

[10] *Manuel d'usage et d'entretien du post-humain*, Dominique Babin, Flammarion, 2004.

over billions of different brains (which maintain a permanent evolution). AI also takes advantage of such an accumulation on the Internet or other databases and algorithms are duly developed to dig into this mass of data.

The ability of a human brain to instinctively make significant relations between concepts which could lead to confusion is presently hardly challenged by machines which are still dominated by a rigid logic even concerning simple events such as those rising in a trivial sentence. For instance, the famous sentence "spirit is ready but flesh is weak" could easily be "understood" by a machine as "the vinegar is served on the table but the meat is of poor quality" if reference is made to a cooking situation. What we call "the common sense" cannot be so easily modeled and translated as an appropriate algorithm in the same way our brain is familiar with, in an instinctive process. There is assuredly no hope to hold out that in a near (or remote) future a computer will be able to provide us with a significant translation of a quatrain from Nostradamus!

This leads to the question whether the human/machine relationship may lead to dramatic mistakes when the two "intelligences" disagree and the machine decides. A real example of such a situation can be given by the crash of a plane some years ago when an Airbus 320, in Habsheim, France was in a demonstration flight at low speed and low flying with landing gear down. All of a sudden there was a stand of high trees in front that had not been pre-empted. The pilot quickly pulled back on the joystick and pushed the thrust levels but the onboard computer was convinced it was in a landing process and did not obey the instructions. The plane crashed causing several human casualties.

A reciprocal aviation situation took place in 2015 with the crash of a similar Airbus in the French Alps following a deliberate morbid suicide wish committed by the co-pilot who locked himself up in the cockpit. The onboard computer was not taught to face such a human problem[11] and did not prevent it. So the question remains: who is to decide in such an ambiguous situation, the man or the machine?[12] The death toll was 144 passengers and crew.

---

[11] A computer does not know the notion of the word "danger".

[12] More recently in March 2019, the computer of a Boeing 737 MAX 8 decided to commit suicide and crashed the plane in spite of the efforts of the pilots to counteract. This raises a similar issue.

These two examples clearly show that giving priority either to the man or the machine is not a clear-cut question and the post-humanists do not suggest any answer. The decision could be left to an external referee, provided that he (it) possesses a very open (and fast) mind. Not so easy ...

This raises the question of consciousness in a computer and its possible ability to stay in relation or in dependence (not to say in symbiosis) with a human brain. Machines are organized as rigidly structured hierarchies of modules, whereas biology is based on holistically organized elements in which every element affects every other. Even if schematically presented, only biological systems can use this design principle. Also of note is that, in a computer, the hardware and the logical set-up are fundamentally distinct entities whereas the brain is not a dualistic entity and is more complicated than simple logic gates; this makes the brain more difficult to upgrade.[13]

We shall deal later and in more details with this very important chapter of the activities of the transhumanists. AI is posed to create miracles in many fields but not yet to challenge a human brain in every domain. That said there is no doubt that pattern recognition, facial expression, or language analysis are currently in a booming growth. Would that be enough for these deterministic methods to compete with the "plasticity" of our spirit?

The subject of AI will be more extensively debated in Chapter 6 but as a primer, suffice it to say that "Strong AI" is known to aim at amplifying what we call human intelligence, thus making reference to the only type of intelligence we know. However, no strategy can absolutely ensure that future AI could embody human ethics and values. "Friendly AI 1.0" has been proposed by Yudkowski[14] to smoothen the "rigidity" of pure logic and "get it right the first time" in such way that the AI design has "zero nonrecoverable errors".

---

[13] "Levels and loops: The future of AI and neuroscience", A J Bell, *Philosophical Transactions of the Royal Society B*, 354, 1999.

[14] *Creating Friendly AI 0.1*, E S Yudkowski, Machine Intelligence Research Institute, 2001. Available at: https://intelligence.org/files/CFAI.pdf

2. Ways of Thinking

Some are convinced that there are good reasons to assume that Science will provide us with a full understanding of the universe that will leave no room for God.[15] However Sean Caroll concedes that "The idea of God has functions other than those of a scientific hypothesis".

In the remote times Gods were at the origin an intellectual creation of the human spirit eager to get an eschatological explanation of his origins and his fate to alleviate his rough life. Is that still so essential and would the computer be taught to understand such an idea?

Today one knows that there is no old man atop of the mountain and that the sky is empty of any divinity. Nevertheless, the Big Bang is still a deep mystery and black matter is still invisible even if we do know it exists somewhere in the skies; so even if science does progresses at a quick pace there are still deep holes in our knowledge and the trend of the trans or post-humanists to "play God" is a bit premature.

2.1. *Transhumanism involvements*

Transhumanism evolves in a surrounding galaxy of centers of interest as suggested in Figure 2.2, with some of the well-known proponents or opponents.

That scattering of multiple links leads to a diversity of approaches, implications and ways of thinking depending on the field concerned. Transhumanism and still more post-humanism maintain a specific and innovative view on all these topics. Like it, hate it, or simply worry about it, that is your choice but nothing has to be rejected *a priori*. Only time will tell us what idea was the right one and strong enough to change our destinies.

These fears of an uncontrolled future have led "Fundamentalists" to turn the clock back on modern ideas and shut down the worrying advances of technology. As the fundamental Luddites, they are claiming precaution-ary principles to confront the existential risks before they appear. Some

---

[15] Sean Caroll, a cosmologist at Caltech: "As we learn more about the universe, there is less and less need to look outside it for help."

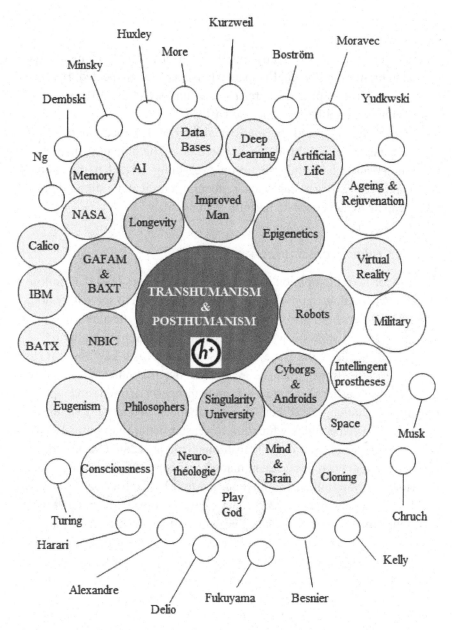

Figure 2.2. Galaxy of the trans- and post-humanism centers of interest and orbiting proponents (or opponents).

also claim that fundamentalists can lead to religious extremism and even terrorism.

They energically refuse any modification of the body or more especially the brain even if a real lifespan extension is duly expected. However the demand for therapies and cures for any illnesses of our 1.0 body prove essential and cannot be discarded so easily.

Max More suggested the implementation of a "proactionary principle" to balance the risk of action or inaction.[16] The humanist theories of the fundamentalists mainly focus on everything related to the human being and especially genetics because there is a need and a strong demand for therapies which could be harmful if misused.

2.2. *The role of consciousness*

Jerry Fodor is of the opinion that: "Some philosophers hold that philosophy is what you do to a problem until it's clear enough to solve it by doing science.[17] Others hold that if a philosophical problem succumbs to empirical methods that shows it wasn't really philosophical to begin with".

More especially, the issue of "consciousness" is a key point of discussion for the transhumanists who face the dilemma of comparing human consciousness (as long as it can be properly defined) and a potential digital challenger. Sergei Brin (co-founder of Google) states that computers "are machines which are to reason better than humans". But is there a matter of "reason"? Transhumanism, as a counterpoint, develops a messianic wish to rescue humanity through a "digital evangelism".

However, throughout my readings on transhumanism I must confess that I only encountered the word "man", never "woman"; would that mean that transhumanists are not concerned with woman or that women are not likely to be "improved"? As a matter of fact the notion of "gender" has currently become a controversial topic. The new perspectives in epigenetics are blurring the future of this natural discrimination and I have not come across any position taken by transhumanism on this issue.

---

[16] "The proactionary principle", Max More, 2004. Available at: http://maxmore.com/proactionary.htm

[17] *RePresentations: Philosophical Essays on the Foundations of Cognitive Science*, Jerry A Fodor, Cambridge Mass: MIT Press, 1981.

3. Are We Bound to Change?

I would better have written: will we still remain human? The changes in our daily lives by invasive technology is already observable: new cures for traditional diseases, noticeable extension of longevity, generalized information (social networks), virtual reality in the media, money replaced by credit card, smartphone invasion, etc. — all of these limited but multiple changes occur at a fast rate and we get accustomed to their involvement in our behaviors. These occur subtly but modify our habits in a significant way; no Singularity was required just an adaptation and we still remain humans even if in some way "modified". We have got to a stage where traveling all over the planet at the speed of sound or even visiting the moon (not yet for everyone) has become commonplace.

3.1. *The change is already here*

The nature of change is a constant and irrepressible evolution from time immemorial. It occurs irrespective of our individual will. Are we bound to think that nothing fundamental will change during our lifetime? Following our guru Kurzweil this is a "narrow view" which is also to change as the implications of the acceleration becomes evident. So change is everywhere even in our minds! We are in a swirl that causes each of us to rethink everything while our ageing processes slow down on a regular basis. This is yet another basic change which occurs outside of our direct perception.

Among the various changes which already sneakily infiltrate our daily behavior and are largely accepted, especially by the Millenials, is the large use of communication; not only the Internet facilities (Whatsapp and the like) but also the travel facilities. This is quite recent but impressive. For instance, every grandparent finds it normal to visit a young boy (or girl as well) who completes a traineeship in a university on the other side of the planet!

3.2. *The age barrier*

The ancient barrier of the hundred years life is now about to fall[18] and the perspective of living beyond 150 years becomes less and less a fanciful

---

[18] *Longevity in the 2.0 World*, Jean Pierre Fillard, World Scientific, 2019.

notion. That is on the way and would not shock anyone; we are mentally ready (even if not socially).

More deep and sudden changes, however, could be expected when decisive steps forward in science or technology will be achieved for all: genetic programing, designer babies, neurological implants, etc. Where could we draw a defining line to separate the "traditional" human from the modified "transhuman"? Our merger with technology has already started and it is hard to decide today where that stops and where eugenism starts. That is the reason why some transhumanists distanced themselves[19] from the term "eugenism" to avoid having their position confused with outdated theories.

This is however not without unpleasant drawbacks; changes and their consequences cannot be welcomed forcibly. This is the back edge of the sword and a cultural rebellion against the unknown is a real worry. This was the case when electricity became of widespread domestic use and even today, when nuclear stations provide it so generously. Such thoughtless anti-technology sentiments have the potential of delaying the progresses, not to stop them.

To what extent do the decisive changes that science is proposing, push us on a trans-human path toward the decisive point of crossing the barrier of a post-human being?

4. Singularity or Singularities

Vernor Vinge[20] was a mathematician and software science specialist who imagined for the first time a Singularity leading to a society of "advanced humans".

The accelerating evolution of 2.0 Science boosts an exploding technology in every domain of knowledge. Each breakthrough in biology suggests new ideas in AI or even in philosophy, each new performing integrated circuit applies to epigenetics as well as to virtual reality. Science and technology have brought all fields of knowledge in a common

---

[19] *Remaking Eden: Cloning and Beyond in a Brave New World*, Silver Lee, Harper Perennial, 1998.

[20] *The Wilting*, Vernor Vinge, Daw, 1976.

web and the Internet allows everybody to contribute even if not a specialist. Everything is related.

4.1. *How Singularity came about*

This recent upheaval has become so bold that some people imagined we are on the edge of a fundamental revolution in our way of living in a world where machines could take a leading role. Ray Kurzweil foresees that we are on the verge of a radical change he called the "Singularity" that would be to come all of a sudden. This word comes from mathematics where it refers to a mathematical function which displays a sharp discontinuity, a rupture in its development.[21] Scientists of the science of materials are familiar with such discontinuities which traditionally describe a definitive rupture following an excessive effort or what is called a "fatigue". Would transhumanists have to submit to such a fatigue to become post-humanists?

The people who are involved in such a reflexion are now called "Singularians". As stated by Kurzweil himself: "a Singularian is someone who understands the Singularity and reflected on its meaning for his (or her) own life". Obviously that sounds, in a manner of speaking, as "a substitute vision for those who have lost faith in the traditional objects of religious beliefs".[22]

However Kurzweil actually defends himself by saying that "being a Singularian is not a matter of faith but one of understanding, pondering the scientific trends I've discussed in this book inescapably engenders new perspectives on the issue of that traditional religions have attempted to address".

For his part, Eliezer Shlomo Yudkowsky argues that "a Singularian is someone who believes that technologically creating a greater-than-human intelligence is desirable, and who works to that end."[23]

---

[21] Not to be confused with an asymptotical hyperbolic limit as stated by Kurzweil.

[22] As mentioned by George Gilder about Kurzweil philosophy of Singularity.

[23] *The Singularitarian Principles*, Eliezer Yudkowsky, 2000. Available at: https://barzha. cyberpunk.us/lib/critica/sing/singprinc.html

All these philosophies rely on the observation that scientific and technological progresses are coming so fast and are so decisive that they are likely to induce fundamental changes in our traditional way of being, in a very short future, whether we want it or not.

Kurzweil produced a plot of time which separated each key event from the following one in the human evolution as a function of the time which separates it from the present time. The data came from a diversity of many observers and reference books which makes that statistic trustworthy.

This convincingly shows, in a logarithmic-logarithmic scale (Figure 2.3.), that there is a steady linear evolution (hyperbolic slope 1) converging

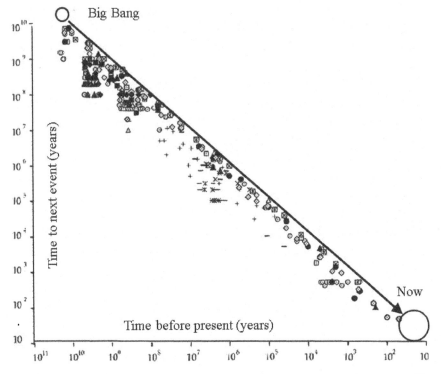

Figure 2.3. Major paradigm shifts as reported by 15 authors after R. Kurzweil.[24]

---

[24] Kurzweil, *Singularity.*

toward the present time for an acceleration of the swiftness of new events. The time delay between decisive events has become so reduced that this behavior inevitably leads to the compression of evolution to a shorter and shorter time.

The extensive geological scale is no longer currently valid. The erratic scattering of the data in the remote times is inevitably due to the limited and inaccurate knowledge of the events at such epochs but things get clearer as we approach the present times and make the plot quite impressive. The hyperbolic behavior in itself does not point specifically to a "singularity" but only to a drastic reduction of the scale of the successive events. This means that decisive events will succeed at such a crazy pace that we will no longer pay attention to them and simply grow accustomed.

The Singularity we are dealing with only refers to a radical human evolution in our being; this remains a continuous evolution even if accelerating in many directions; there is no rupture in the processing. An important point is also to determine if these changes will imply everybody or only the most "adapted" ones. The answer is not so clear if we consider the particular current phenomenon of the global smartphone extension. Another more speculative question could be: would the Big Bang itself have been a Singularity in a "multiverse" context?

This plot also confirms and extends what we have already explained in the previous chapter concerning the triggering role of the discovery of new forms of energy. The delays shorten inexorably toward something new we cannot presently precisely describe; call it Singularity or otherwise.

We are now bound to undergo a real deluge of innovations that will require reconsidering our basic behaviors. In the mind of Kurzweil this will be a single event triggered by a single discovery. This event could likely be a super AI development. Others are more pessimistic such as Vernor Vinge,[25] a famous science fiction author, who states that this intelligence would grow so quickly that it would result in the end of the era for human civilization.

---

[25] "The Coming Technological Singularity: How to Survive in the Post-Human Era", Vernor Vinge, 1993. Available at: https://edoras.sdsu.edu/~vinge/misc/singularity.html

4.2. *Is Singularity for real?*

The general process of such a Singularity is conveniently described in the sketch provided by Marco Alpini[26] (Figure 2.4.). This author considers that the collapse of a Singularity induced by a self-improving AI is only part of a bigger story which implies linked consequences following other accelerating trends: evolutionary, technical, ecological Singularities. The threshold represented here is rather smooth, not really a sharp rupture as in a genuine Singularity.

The occurrence of such a Singularity in our daily human life[27] (as emphasized by Kurzweil) would certainly apply simultaneously in many domains: the human body (blood, heart, brain, muscles … and their digital versions), the life expectation, or the ways of learning (deep?). You may

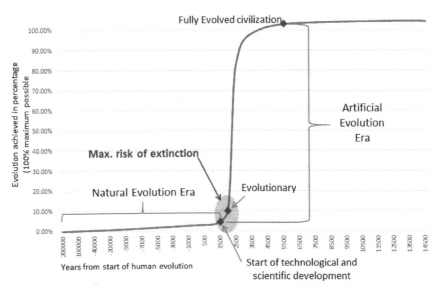

Figure 2.4.   A sketch of the occurrence of a Singularity process.

---

[26] "Does Evolution lead to Singularity?", Marco Alpini, *Singularity Weblog*, November 12, 2015. Available at: https://www.singularityweblog.com/does-evolution-lead-to-singularity/
[27] Supposing this could concern at least a majority of us.

note that most of these topics are already on the way without waiting for a hypothetical Singularity.

Our servitude has nevertheless already been openly achieved by the big companies: Samsung, Google, IBM and some others in a watered-down but psychologically intrusive form known as "entrepreneurial spirit". The aim being to improve productivity, they initiated a familial "cocooning" very close to a pre-established mind model to be accepted.[28]

Following Kurzweil, computation power is key to impart a decisive advantage for AI over human intelligence. This implies other difficulties inherent with an abnormal upsizing of the computer. The year he foresees for a disruptive singularity triggered by an overcapacity of computers could by estimated in the 2045 range.

Obviously all of that should be based on a convincing definition of "intelligence" which is not so easy to achieve even with a performing computer! By the way, it would be worth using the word intelligence in the plural form; there actually are so many variants in the meaning of this word! On top of that, intelligence means understanding but it does not mean power to do.

Kurzweil himself has developed a distinction between information and knowledge which is at the origin of intelligence: "we have hundreds of megabits of information flowing through our senses every second, the bulk of which is intelligently discarded. It is only the key recognitions and insights (all forms of knowledge) that we retain. Thus intelligence selectively destroys information to create knowledge".

Singularity theories (or phantasm, some would say) generated much criticism especially concerning the technological acceleration which is considered at the very root of the problem. In particular is the criticism that such theories do not take into account the considerable needs in energy. AI proceeds from machine and machines never work for free, they need energy then they will necessarily remain dependent on humans who alone can manage energy. The higher performing the machines, the more energy they require (even using Moore's law to predict an explosive development of submicronic integrated circuits). Data centers are known to be especially bulimic in energy to the point they are put in a place located not far from a power station.

---

[28] *Brain versus Computer*, Jean Pierre Fillard, World Scientific, 2017.

4.3. *A world of machines?*

It is a very unrealistic point of view to imagine a world where machines could be so intelligent and powerful as to find and put into action a source of energy and corresponding resources, in the long run and by themselves. Remember the "death" of Hal in the film "Space Odysseus" when Dave pulled the plug out of its power supply? To become a real danger for humanity the machines would also need to have the ability to reproduce by themselves (as human does from eternity and up to now) and that is not for tomorrow even if they would become "intelligent" enough.

However this necessity of reproduction stems from our human scheme of a biological life limited by birth on one side and death on the other. Such a scheme may not be valid for a machine which could support itself, being unique or distributed in several places in order to escape any physical aggression or breakdown. The undisputable advantage of the machine over the human brain is that a machine can transfer his information (knowledge) in a jiffy whereas a human brain usually requires 30 years!

In previous centuries energy was the trigger for the emergence of new civilizations but today the 2.0 civilization does not propose any new species of energy. The power of decision still remains in the hands of man. This supports the idea that there could not be "a" Singularity but may be several limited ones restricted to specific domains under a direct human control. Some say that the Singularians are more likely believers than real scientists. Others dare say that Kurzweil is no more than a "charlatan".

Nevertheless Singularity typically would take place in the material world, not in a quantum virtuality of incertitude. That does not prevent encounters of transcendence and spirituality precisely in this material world. It is the presence and the power of these "patterns" (as said by Kurzweil) that are at the very basis of human intelligence that surges from the deepness of the brain. We call this immaterial but materially supported matter "consciousness".

Of course, machines (at least for the time being) are deprived from such a "facility" even if they assuredly become more and more intelligent following a "machina sapiens" path suggested by Hans Moravec. Might it (one day) be conceivable that a machine could access this source of inventiveness, creativity, emotions, beauty, sensitivity and so turning dumb matter into a proper intelligence able to challenge (and, maybe, replace) the human one? Would that necessarily be associated with sensations or sentiments like love, fear, pain (or hate and anger)?

Does all of that entail that this opportunity to "go beyond" would be the essential prerequisite to the triggering of this Singularity Kurzweil is waiting for? But for how long would such a process be a result of randomness or rational good science? Would such an advanced machine remain a deterministic one or would it will get "personalized" and live its own life if a possibility of acting has been conferred upon it (he?)?

Max More[29] worries about a "cultural rebellion" against hubris and the unknown of technology but also realizes that previous important events in the 20th century such as wars (cold or not) did not slow down the technological progression. Conversely, the reverse was the case. And Bill Gates echoes : "We need a charismatic leader for this new religion. Okay, a charismatic computer then!" and added afterwards: "Oh, it will be conscious; I just think it will be a different type of consciousness … because computers can merge together instantly … as human, we can't do that".

All of that considered, it is yet unknown how such an abrupt transition could take place in societies which are not yet prepared to mute. The human condition is so largely diversified that it will take time to explain to people what is going to be done. Some would follow, others won't. Would the change be for free or would it require a substantial voluntary contribution? The issue is not like buying a smartphone!

It would be likely that, at the beginning at least, there would be experimental trials to check the feasibility of the transformation. This will necessarily take time; there is no magic wand. We know we are able to go to the moon but this is not appropriate for everyone.

Also, with the ongoing process and supposing that the fabrication of "improved men" would work satisfactorily, would not these first privileged individuals take advantage of their new "intelligence" to impose a kind of dictatorship over the "less gifted"? Would these improved men

---

[29] "Max More and Ray Kurzweil on the Singularity", Max More and Ray Kurzweil, Kurzweil accelerating intelligence, February 26, 2002. Available at: https://www.kurzweilai.net/max-more-and-ray-kurzweil-on-the-singularity-2

be of a single standard model or would they be diversified and keep a "personality"?

As a matter of fact transhumanism deals with the future scientific opportunities to "change the Man" but humanity is made of Men and today they look somewhat disparate at a national scale and even more so at a global scale. However, transhumanists already benefit from very good arguments and also very large means provided as well in the US or in China to promote their philosophy. Who can remain indifferent (among other pledges) to the perspective of becoming "rejuvenated" and able to live much longer in good shape?

Entire national or political societies are involved in such a "no return" movement: military, industry, health cares as well as ... business of course! This shows the magnitude of the implications.

Chapter Three

New Ways of Life

Today there are two paths to "Transhumanism"; two paths that seek to meet together (and sometimes slightly overlap) but still remain separated: the biological track (brain, genomics, stem cells, etc.) and the mineral one (computing, robotics, AI, etc.). Which one will be the first to "improve" Man? Nobody yet knows but spectacular events are inevitable that could someday lead to fundamental change. Perhaps all it takes is the right technological click.

1. The Gurus of the Future and the Augmented Man

One possible trigger could come from the ongoing advances reached in the computer analysis of human thought. Relying on robotics, there are good arguments along this line: to help the disabled (exoskeleton), ease the burden of workers (handling, gathering agricultural products, etc.), replace soldiers (there is where money can be found). The bottleneck at the moment is a convenient man/machine interface to control the robots. A satisfactory way of connecting the neuron to electronics has yet to be found. However we are making headway in learning how to interpret brain waves and that could be a convenient shortcut to begin with.

1.1. *The gurus have come*

Today the "gurus of the future" are back with arguments that are more impressive. Science keeps bringing new discoveries to our thesaurus of knowledge in every domain. It is not surprising that the modern-day Pythias are often patented scientists from biology and computing. This is not a matter of a cult of fanatics, or a sect. The Singularity University teaches pragmatic methods of work to industrial or economy executives in any discipline to anticipate global opportunities because "business is business"!

Reasonable forecasting is essential for industrial companies to anticipate the rapid evolution of the business. Twenty years ago Kodak held a global monopoly in the photographic film business but their managers were unaware of the onset of the digital age. This big company collapsed in a few years' time, due to lack of responsiveness. In another example, IBM initially did not trust in the future of the personal computer. The dazzling success of the Macintosh (Apple) awakened the giant but it was too late.

Such progress has not always been recognized nor accepted; it is still the subject of a natural reluctance, even a fear of adopting innovation as long as it is not required or originating from elsewhere. So the "gurus" often make wild predictions and it takes time for their predictions to be ultimately accepted (when this happens!).

So, inexorably, computers, and corresponding gurus of "Dataism", will face the idea of God which so obsesses the human mind. Would the machine make a choice for a referenced religion or will it process all of them in parallel ... or will it make, here too, an "intelligent optimized synthesis" of them[1] to keep a satisfactory relationship with every human? Even the famous French surgeon, geneticist, businessman, essayist Laurent Alexandre does not approach the matter; GAFA (Google, Apple, Facebook, Amazon) is not interested neither is Alibaba; they want to impose their own laws and show demiurgic impulse with the idea of re-creating the world! Never mind, the religions also have their gurus who have been followed!

1.2. Medicine and genetics

Obviously medicine and genetics are the most advanced fields where the challenge of the gurus countering the idea of God is most severe because the new knowledge of the biological constitution of man reaches a limit

---

[1] *Homo Deus, A Brief History of Tomorrow*, Yuval Noah Harari, Harvil Secker London, 2015.

where unexpected actions become accessible which were considered, up to now, so unthinkable that they were referred to belong only to the realm of God. We shall come back to this important subject later.

Up until now knowledge was accumulated in human memories or safeguarded in memory repositories such as manuscripts, books or encyclopedias to be preserved and possibly retrieved. These progresses were of a considerable importance in the evolution of civilizations but they remained quite limited due to the huge scale of the issue. That role is now shared with computers and their inexhaustible memories can store a wealth of data on a very much larger scale.

The size of the memories in data centers is such that the corresponding medical techniques and cures to fight identified diseases can be located despite the complexity of the human body. This provides us with unprecedented opportunities to help the physician get a safe diagnosis and counsel an adapted medical treatment to the patient. This astonishing prospect goes so far that, at the very limit, some may ask if the physician does remain a necessary intermediary if the machine is able to solve the situation on its own; such a situation, of course, shall require an advanced AI to search for the best path. The transhumanists are fond of such a debate! The pinnacle of AI is to become fully autonomous; however, hopefully, we are not yet there and the doctor still retains the ultimate control[2] over the machine even if its assistance will remain of an invaluable help.

Pharmacology now gathers thousands of drugs which selectively aim at curing a specific disease. This is a rather simplistic view because every disease is multifaceted, especially when genetics is to play a role. It appears now that the computer is the very and only tool to find a way in the complexity of the drug action or interaction when several of them are simultaneously required. The trend now is to use AI to get to a personalized and even predictive medicine. Genomics has yielded kinds of medical breakthrough that many innovators hoped for. But it has been shown that a single gene[3] has the capacity to have multiple and seemingly unrelated effects thus leading to a complexity called "pleiotropy".

---

[2] "Cardiologist Eric Topol on How AI Can Bring Humanity Back to Medicine", Alice Park, *Time*, March 2019. Available at: https://time.com/collection/life-reinvented/5551296/cardiologist-eric-topol-artificial-intelligence-interview/

[3] "Finding new cures in old drugs", Ray Tiernan, *Fortune*, April 1, 2019.

Great expectations are fueled by AI performances to find a valuable therapy for Alzheimer's, Parkinson's, or Amyotrophic Lateral Sclerosis (ALS) and even Cancer, using repurposed combination of drugs to face the influence of several combined genes and take into account the many differences occurring from patient to patient. Complicated diseases often are confluences of numerous effects because a given protein can act at different places in the body and with different functions, not only one; the AI assisted computer is the only possible recourse to dig into the data-bases and find an adjusted therapy. This is the very dawn of the modern genetic research which transhumanists are calling for.

This could lead to new concepts and deep changes for the pharmaceu-tical industry that will be called to produce "on request" computer designed medications instead of the wide spectrum drugs as is currently the case today.

2. Knowledge: A Shared Collective Behavior

For millennia, knowledge was accumulated until the present 2.0 world where an explosive dimension has been reached. We no longer need to wait a long while before finding the right information we are looking for; a simple click on the Internet gives rise to a profusion of suggestions on the monitor screen! So we are doomed to communicate with the machine and share its intimacy. Knowledge has become a deep mine we have to dig in.

2.1. *The dialogue with the machine*

This is currently achieved through mouse and keyboard and the machine answers through the screen of a monitor regardless whether it is a com-puter or smartphone. That works fine but remains quite primitive a process and not so intimate in front of the irrepressible curiosity of Google and Co.

Let us imagine that, soon, we would be able to confidently and directly speak (and think) with the machine simply using an electronic cap on the head. This begins to be conceivable, at least in the way brain > machine, as of now. This is only a technological problem and a solution will certainly arise one day; many people are working on this topic around the world.

The transhumanists are fond of such a direct dialogue but what may happen the day when such a "two way" relation will be feasible? Assuredly the computer will do its job well: it searches, finds, memorizes, learns, and perfects itself. It will become familiar with its human interlocutor in order to provide a better and faster answer. One can say that the machine will rummage in the brain and permeate the personality of its willing partner who no longer becomes a simple correspondent. One can easily imagine that this lack of intimacy would benefit a prospect of neuro-marketing (already active on Internet) or even a kind of brainwashing; Big Brother would directly enter our head! On top of that the human interlocutor could get a taste of it and abandon his smartphone in favor of the bonnet! Who will become the slave of the other?

2.2. A machine or the "cloud"?

There is no requirement for the computer to be a physical machine but it could become virtual somewhere in the "cloud" and thus cannot be unplugged as it was the case for Hal.[4] The moment will come when the machine will know almost everything about its human partner and will train itself by imitating its "friend" to the point it will become uneasy to discriminate between the brain and the machine.

Then the computer (which is faster than the neurons) could (why not?) begin to impose its foolproof logic by suggesting its own ideas that will be accepted. One gets to a point where the human loses any initiative and surrenders to a greater intelligence than himself. What will be to happen when the man dies? The computer will not stop there; it will continue alone if, meanwhile, the biologists do not discover the secret of an eternal life! All of that is in no way science fiction but a possible science.

3. Transhumanism 2.0 Versus Religions

The "idea of God" has been raised for millennia and many "models" have been elaborated, which entered our lives and can be easily approached: we call them religions.

---

[4] In the 2001 film by Stanley Kubrick, *A Space Odyssey*.

As Sean Carroll (a cosmologist at Caltech) puts it: "as we learn more about the universe, there is less and less need to look outside it for help". This, of course, is a totally gratuitous statement which can obviously be challenged.

Simple observation assisted by science required millenaries to understand that God is neither a caring old man with a long white beard sitting atop a mountain or behind a cloud in the skies, nor a furious warrior sending lightning. However, such intellectual constructions were required from the beginning to provide men with strong social links and address any metaphysical concern.

3.1. *Today, the knowledge*

Today enormous progress has been made on the knowledge of our human condition; some say that humanity is to drastically change with the emergence of "transformed", "repaired", or even "improved", or "enhanced" men; this to the point that some uncontested prerogatives attributed to the divine are now to be challenged although, however, the ultimate mystery of our being here still remains unsolved.

Then a question comes: in the light of current discoveries, would we now have to consider deeply changing our minds? Would the idea of God be doomed to vanish in the human mind after milleniums of good and loyal (?) faith? Would we have to concentrate on pure rationality and the new possible ways of being that technology is to offer? Would all humans be able to take the leap of 2.0 or would there be a necessary "natural" selection of them? That constitutes a lot of questions!

What is going to happen with the increasing knowledge of our world today? What could be the effects of the rising "rationality" of the computer? Some still say that the machine is definitely stupid, deterministic and never could challenge the subtle imagination of the human mind. However it is indisputable that as the computer becomes more and more "intelligent", it would begin to "think" and be intuitive. On top of that, the machine is currently able to handle a huge mass of data a human mind could never manage. What could happen to the idea of God in such a context? Would such an idea become obsolete? Transhumanists are rather reluctant to consider their "philosophy" as a religion.

3.2. *The conflict*

Traditionally, Science has been viewed with some degree of hostility by the religions because it brings indisputable evidences which are unattainable by the religions.

Richard Dawkins[5] is a famous biologist trained in a pure Oxfordian religious education which did not predispose him to such a challenging role of transhumanist. He gave many other publications, conferences, contributions in public debates, and so on. For instance, detailed discussions were also reported by John Brockman[6] with the contribution of Craig Venter, Ray Kurzweil, George Church, and other transhumanist celebrities.

Dawkins claims he is a committed atheist but he also thinks he has to convince himself because of his irreducible religious education. The center of the debate is: are we to agree that God exists? This comment of Dawkins is rather skewed or foolish: "I shall suggest that the existence of God is a scientific hypothesis".

This brings us to the case of the "digital information" which would be engraved in our personal DNA. This might be a God's language we are not (yet) able to fully decipher; the syntactic message is readily got but we still miss the semantic.

Are genes to belong to a God's language to specify their behavior? What could be the "specified complexity"[7] of such a language? How to imagine the moving from simple molecules to an organized DNA?

Science never aimed at finding out who is God. Science is in no way at war with God; Science doesn't care; it is not a delusion.

Then would it not become possible that the "transformed Men" simply omit the idea of God and classifies it in the category of scientifically unexplained phenomena?

With the coming of the "self-driving car" it has become mandatory to teach the computer how to follow the Code. It will also be mandatory to teach the android-bot to obey a sort of religion in order for it to behave in

---

[5] *The God Delusion*, Richard Dawkins, Black Swan, 2006.
[6] *Life*, John Brockman, ed., Harper Perennial, 2016.
[7] *The Origin of Life*, Lesly Orgel, NY Wiley, 1973.

a civic way when in a human society. Religion cannot be dissociated from the society whatever it is. No matter the religion, we live in the framework of seven days a week as specified by the Bible.

Religion is no longer of a major metaphysical essential concern. Technology and the quest for comfort and individual welfare have grown in its place. However, the main unquestionable prerogatives of God are still not affected: life, death, or intelligence still remain mysteries, but perhaps not for a long time.

3.3. The arguments

Van Leuwenhoek discovered the incredible microscopic world (still then completely unknown) of the "animalcules" among which were the spermatozoids. As a result of his invention — the microscope (somewhat a small magnifying ball of glass!) — the myth of the God's sovereign power in procreation slowly vanishes in front of the compelling scientific evidence the microscope has revealed.

Today the boom takes place in every scientific domain and religion will have to revise its basic principles and accept adjustments, especially in the field of Biology and procreation: Contraceptive pill, Abortion (VPI), Gestational Surrogacy, Voluntary Interruption of Pregnancy (VTP), Pre-Implant Diagnosis (PID), all current initiatives which run counter to the established religious principles and trigger religious hostility.

At the very beginning the world has been created for us especially by God (this in an anthropic Christian view) and it was classified into two categories: the inanimate mineral things (the Earth, the sky, the seas, the stones, etc.) and the living species (the beasts, the fishes, the birds, the plants, etc.) and this very special animal: the Man who was, in particular, gifted a soul!

However, in these remote times, a new species has appeared between the two previous established ones: the "artifacts" which refers to objects directly artificially created by human craftsmanship to play a role in his life and his evolution (see Figure 3.1); so appeared knifes, axes, and various other manufactured goods. Jacques Monod[8] distinguished between

---

[8] *Le hasard et la nécessité*, Jacques Monod, Ed du Seuil, 1970.

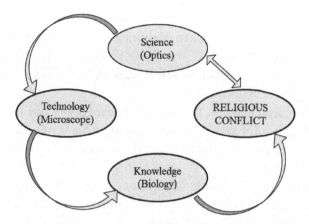

Figure 3.1. Typical sketch of evolution following Van Leuwenhoek.

natural objects and artifacts in order to say that artifacts are a direct production of craftsmanship and carry with them the "project" of an action.
It is due to the artifacts that humanity has been able to progress so largely
for millennia.

Today the acquired knowledge about our human condition has greatly
improved; some argue that humanity is on the verge of a drastic change with
the emergence of transformed, repaired, improved, reinforced new men —
to the point that the main prerogatives of the divine are already challenged
although the ultimate mystery of our existence remains unanswered.

Then comes the question: in the light of the current discovery, would
we also have to change our mind deeply? Would the idea of God be
intended to vanish from the human minds after millennia of loyal (?!)
services? Would we have to turn to pure rationality and the new ways of
life technology is going to bring about? Are all humans ready to jump
into the 2.0 world or would we be forced to make a drastic "selection"
among them?

The first biblical recommendation ("thou shall not kill") remains of
prime importance (even if not strictly obeyed!) and deserves to be preserved as a priority. If the idea of God disappears (and the notion of basic
morale too), would the social peace still be conceivable? If Man, as well
as the robots, has to be "improved" that would be the first demand to be
taken into account in the Turing requirements.

Globalization allows different religions that, up to recently, were, more or less, located in dedicated territories and specified populations to come into contact. "In God we trust" still remains printed as a hallmark on the American currency but, now, one is entitled to wonder who is "We" and what "God" is concerned.

As Sean Caroll[9] puts it, "the more we learn about our universe, the less we feel a need for seeking aid elsewhere". This is of course a gratuitous assertion in line with transhumanist philosophy and so could obviously be contested.

However, very soon, some like Moses or the Hebrew Prophets condemned these habits of challenging Nature; however, at the same time, the Greek philosophers (Thales or Xenophanes) also denounced the vision of a mythological world, saying that such fictions were childish. Such heretical reactions can still be observed among transhumanist theory supporters.

As the living species mute and change with time, so have the religions deeply evolved (or bluntly disappeared) from the beginning even if each of them claims that it represents the only belief worthy to be followed. Turbulent wars often accompanied these changes.

Sterile debates have been proposed from time to time such as the famous one about the rotation of the Earth and following Galileo's "abdication" ("*e pur si muove!*"). However among the many branches of the Science tree, two of them get closer to the religious space: biology, which implicates the basic process of life (and death), and AI which begins to challenge the brain itself but is not a new insight, for centuries Science underlined conclusions that are not consistent with previous religious statements.

3.4. *Transhumanism atheism and neurotheology*

Transhumanism is a modern extension[10] of the "postmodernism" theory which aimed for a long time to take into account the prospects of a disruption in our way of life induced by enhancing technology. From the 16th

---

[9] A cosmologist at Caltech who is famous for his atheist position. See: https://en.wikipedia.org/wiki/Sean_M._Carroll?oldid=384324220

[10] *The Unbearable Wholeness of Being*, Ilia Delio, Orbis Books, 2013.

century Science has been contradicting with religion but did not succeed in establishing a trustworthy convenient model in this realm; Theihard de Chardin was the only philosopher trying to open a meditation on science and culture in the quest for the secrets of life; he was rejected by Roma. Now, because of the speed at which things change, transhumanism attempts to shine some light on a possible future. Would Ray Kurzweil be a modern version of a prophet?

Aldous Huxley was the first to use the word Neurotheology[11] in 1962, later followed by Laurence O. McKinney.[12] This was a questioning about the possible relationship between the growing knowledge of the brain mechanisms and the idea of God. Of course the performing instruments 2.0 provide us, largely encourage inquisitiveness and Louis Pasteur was right and premonitory when saying: "a little science distracts from God; much draws us closer". In these times, scientific research mostly relied on the subconscious intuition rather than the rationality which now prevails.

These researches are part of a wider domain called "cognitics" which aims to explore the external physicochemical influences and identify a possible "place of God" in the brain. Would there be a biological, congenital origin? Where could this idea be hidden? It has effectively been established that meditation notably increases the blood flux in some front circumvolutions in the temporal lobe; but is meditation exclusively dedicated to God?

There is currently an extensive literature, many discussions and various experimental explorations about the subject, but without reaching any clear indication. Andrew B. Newberg[13] states that "our MRI cerebral experiments will never demonstrate the existence nor the non-existence of God; that is not the purpose." Nevertheless some consider neurotheology as a possible universal virtual religion[14] for the future and a substitute for the previous ones.

---

[11] *Île*, Aldous Huxley, ed., 1962.

[12] *Neurotheology: Virtual Religion in the 21ˢᵗ Century*, Laurence O. McKinney, American Institute for Mindfulness, 1994.

[13] *Principles of Neurotheology*, A. B. Newberg, Ashgate Pub Co., 2010.

[14] McKinney, *Neurotheology*.

Nevertheless, efforts are developed to identify, by EEG and electromagnetic stimulation, the cerebral origin of the religious feeling. One would have demonstrated that it would originate in the circumvolution of the front lobe of the brain where an innate religious sentiment could be located that would predispose man to trust in God.[15] Is that really innate or would it be acquired in the very early lifetime of the baby as an external influence? As a matter of fact brain is not an organ as simple as the others!

As an example of the radio waves' influence on the brain, investigations were performed on the "mood". Mood is a vague feeling which goes from daydream to ecstasy and could accompany the idea of God. This mood can be influenced by a propitious environment of images, sounds and especially infra-sounds. It is accompanied by a noticeable increase of blood stream in the brain. Several devices of external electrical brain stimulation are commercially available[16] to "regulate the mood as one regulates the living room temperature" as Amy Webb (Webbmedia)[17] tells us. No scientific explanation has been proposed on how that works nor on the possible secondary effects of such a "cerebral fitness coaching". Despite these evident drawbacks, they are still selling well!

If the catholic religion stays very skeptical with respect to neurotheology because of its affirmed dogma, it is not the same for Buddhism which ignores the notion of God as presented by the Christians. Their spiritual authorities, including the Dalai Lama himself, are open to collaboration with science and do not formulate criticisms against transhumanism.

3.5. The conflict

"Religions" were born in the prehistorical caves with the first hominids 100,000 years ago, because of the worrying mystery of these places they were obliged to live in. Meditation, fear, contemplation were enhanced later with the wall paintings and the first "divinities" appeared with the Homo Sapiens around 10,000 BC in the Middle East and elsewhere. This

---

[15] "Are children intuitive theists?", D Keleman, *Psychological Science XV N°5*, 2004.

[16] Some brands include: Narbis, Melon, Melomind, etc.

[17] https://futuredayinstitute.com

shows that the environment is a stimulating psychological induction to a religious mystic believing.

In these remote times and to keep wild animals at bay, people used to live in caves some of which were very deep and obscure. This mysterious atmosphere favored meditation especially when sounds were produced that echoed in the flickering light of the torches. Rupert Till, an archeologist[18] from the University of Huddensfield (United Kingdom), reconstituted such "music" with recovered instruments (horns, bones that were whirled on a string, and so on). This atmosphere helped reach a state of mystic contemplation which accompanied tribal rites. Same thing nowadays in many (if not every) religions!

The mystery of death also stimulated believing in the same way and induced the creation of funeral ceremonies and corresponding paintings, tombs, arts, and ornaments. These recipes still hold valid in every church, cathedral, synagogue, or shrine with statues, paintings, music, songs, and even perfumes to help reach a collective contemplative state.

More especially it was recognized that sounds and notably infrasounds play a key role in accessing the second state of meditation. So behave the horns which accompany the prayers in the extreme-oriental religions or the organs in Occident, to contribute to a conditioning. This external interaction with the brain is carefully studied today by neurophysiologists as an open access to the unconscious.

Richard Wiseman[19] (so appropriately named) wanted to know more; he built a 7 meters long infra-sound gun to fire on 750 human volunteers; 22% of these human "guinea-pigs" reported strange sensations, goosebumps, and retrieved repressed painful memories. All of that was displayed with an increased heart rate.

Not to invoke drug's effects on the mind, smells can also play a positive role in achieving bliss. Incense is the most famous of these fragrances and universally accepted for its property to accompany meditation and prayers.

---

[18] "Q&A: Acoustic Archaeologist", Rupert Till, *Nature*, Feb 2014. Available at: https://www.researchgate.net/publication/260169632_QA_Acoustic_archaeologist
[19] Richard Wiseman is a professor at the University of Hertfordshire.

All of this, however, still remains purely empirical, instinctive, and without any precise scientific justification. "2.0" has not yet allowed discovering God's spot in the brain!

3.6. *The arguments*

Quantum gravity theory is an attempt to get an explanation of what the time notion could have been before the Big Bang. Was there a need for a supernatural jumpstart or just a "transitional stage in an eternal universe" (Caroll)? Was there a multi-universe? Hopefully "the idea of God has functions other than those of a scientific hypothesis": a societal glue that motivates people to follow collective rules. Would that glue dissolve with growing opportunities of knowledge and how people could be linked in a same society?

The more recent advance in biology is assuredly the CRISPR process (which is nothing more than a natural process for bacteria). The inventors, Jennifer Doudna and Emmanuelle Charpentier said: "having this technology enables humans to alter human evolution" and " CRISPR technology allows to easily and inexpensively find and alter any piece of DNA in any species. Worldwide race will push the limits of capabilities."[20] This powerful technology is on the verge of being actively explored all over the planet but in some way could result in putting us on "a slippery slope".[21] This is also strong support for the transhumanism philosophy.

4. Innovations of Any Kind

Scientific innovations induce technical devices or instruments that are to directly play a role in our individual way of life; that comes from every kind of domain.

4.1. *Biological domain*

As stated by Francis Collins of the National Institute of Health, innovation is "[t]he beginning of a kind of medicine that stands to effectively change

---

[20] "Electrifying Medicine", Alice Park, *Time*, December 19, 2016.

[21] "U.S. Panel Endorses Designer Babies to Avoid Serious Disease", Antonio Regalado, *MIT Technology* Review, February 14, 2017. Available at: https://www.technologyreview.com/s/603633/us-panel-endorses-designer-babies-to-avoid-serious-disease/

the course of human history". For the first time, genetically modified children could be acceptable in narrow circumstances (to avoid serious diseases), according to National Academy of Sciences.[22] Some say that prevention is not enhancement and it could be considered as a "procreative liberty" similarly for abortion. Modified twin girls were already created by a Chinese biologist to prevent them from a risk of getting HIV due to her father's heredity. Last I noticed, they are doing well!

A tricky question could be formulated regarding the cell's behavior: would there be a kind of intelligence at the cellular level which could manage their life and their evolution? Such "cognitive" properties would stray from pure determinism. The very role of proteins is not yet clear: is their constitution really an element of chance? Nevertheless, from bacteria to animals, the chemical machinery is essentially the same in terms of structures as well as operation.

The technological revolution along with the corresponding societal revolution induces deep changes in domestic life, relocation, offshoring and work obligations for women. The biggest impact could be expected on the Islamic religious concept. A certain amount of hypocrisy is starting to emerge with the inevitable incompatibility of religion with modern realities: it is no longer Allah who guides conduct but Man. This is to be implicitly accepted out of necessity even if it does not fit with the basic religious principles.

4.2. The digital domain

Now the digital domain is to invade our daily life by means of connected objects. We are already hounded by Big Brother (BB) on multiple fronts.

The hype around this intelligent technology has peaked[23] and, as the new AI guru Andrew Ng (from Baidu) puts it: "AI is the new mobile, the new electricity", the future commerce SoLoMo (Social, Local, Mobile) is taking place. Mindsets slowly change, and starting with the youth, so is the idea of God.

Now the Internet of Things (IoT) is taking care of you, the individual intimacy is over whether you like it or not. God is no longer almighty, now it's AI.

---

[22] Ibid.

[23] Erin Griffith, *Fortune*, March 25, 2017.

- The smartphone has become an unfathomable source of personal data. Smartphone applications thrive with more and more "fluid" targets. One such example is Snapchat. This platform is unreachable on the Web for simple people but its access requires to be "initiated". Nothing is anymore explained; you have to previously know about and keep intuitive in the dialogue with the computer. However this free instant messaging application allows temporary transfers of images or videos.
- Self-driving car is able to provide BB with every datum about your driving habits and addresses which can be correlated with previously obtained smartphone data to lead to a coherent profile of your personal life. It is emphasized that such a monitoring could induce an efficient speed control and in a traffic violation case an immediate payment of a fine through your credit card!
- Connected objects invade your last private space: your home. The Home PC is no longer alone, now your microwave oven is able to tell BB what exactly your cooking habits are, whereas your watch will inform it about your health. All of that is designed to bring you a new level of convenience and instant assistance but at the same time the data will also be largely appreciated by others, less well-intentioned, such as your supermarket or your insurance company and many others.

5. Collective Behavior

Big companies like IBM or GE do not attract the young talented ambitious people which regard them as obsolete. These people turn to Google, Facebook, or "sexy upstarts like Snapchat"; so mature mega-companies are investing heavily in "employer branding" to market their companies to job seekers. Millennials are now looking for hipster organizations that reflect their personal values (Airbnb, Pinterest, Snap) and local competence. The company no longer makes a choice among the youth to hire but the contrary now holds, the target being becoming skilled at intelligent computing. The dialogue is open with "thinking computers". Everything enters the turmoil.

Religions impose rules which are to be respected among society and this leads to a kind of imperialism based on faith and not rationale; this attitude cannot sustain for long in our world where logic and reasoning are essential.

So divergences ineluctably appear. A gap is generated with nothing to fill it, up to now. Knowledge and intelligence belong to only a few people who are able to maintain balance. With globalization, the frightening rate of social changes and the mixing of different convictions makes it harder for people to evolve at the same pace and at the same standards. Would everything be able to be assimilated and standardized in so short a while?

Obviously the human brain capacity cannot be freely extended; the new elements required by the 2.0 world have to find an adapted arrangement between the neurons and this is obtained at the expense of previous knowledge which are now considered useless. This is a pity that culture is often affected by "what is useless" and has been thrown away. See Figure 3.2.

Yet until a century ago the societies in the developed world were still directed by a few "educated" people who were more or less in a common coherent behavior whereas others "non-favored" were not so largely concerned and had to be guided by intuitive rules. Today, because of the

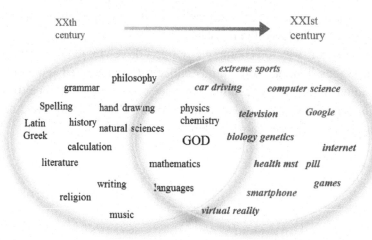

Figure 3.2. Recent changes in culture.

massive diffusion of the instruction (not so much education) everybody got, at school or at university, a minimum standard package of instruction allows each person to express his opinion even if his intellectual means are not that bright (call them poor, dumb, or "schmucks", that does not matter). They really democratically came to power in any domain from policy to ... even "culture" !

Everybody is granted a degree at school or university but not necessarily the corresponding knowledge. The modern communication means allow everybody to communicate and express their views ... and so they do.

Effectively these people have become the dominant voice in the "democratic" societies even if they have not yet reached the ability to voice. Television is currently democratically conducted by the ratings and may be the reason why the TV shows have become so dramatically poor intellectually during the last decade.

Human minds are of a limited volume and culture content has drastically changed; religion (and corresponding "morale") has been completely pushed aside. Many more important priorities have merged. This is accompanied by a rising contestation which, in the ancient times was restrained by religion which had the force of law in curbing violent impulses. Schmucks (and the others) followed the rules without argument, for fear they would be sent to hell. Today God's law no longer induces fear (except in Islam, perhaps) in the face of the omnipresent technology. The handset has replaced the missal.

We are on the way to becoming e-puppets driven by job requirements. New messages dominate our minds and must be accepted without any discussion as long as new "priests" have decided of the truth to be trusted in. So is the case with "global warming", rising CO_2 emissions and other warnings certified by so-called experts.

Chapter Four

Favorite Goals of Transhumanists

Among the many innovations that Science provides us with in the rising 2.0 world, some of them are especially appreciated by the transhumanists and have induced unfathomable perspectives for humanity (or at least some). This has given rise to a movement of thought referred to[1] as "a philosophy" centered on particular goals which are considered as fundamentally involved in the expected future for the whole of humanity.

1. The Transhumanist Philosophy

Transhumanism is in no way a philosophy *stricto sensu*, although it is a source of constant chatter for a swarm of philosophers. Scientists are not directly involved in the discussions but more likely in the possible consequences or extensions of their discoveries. Despite the risky extrapolations, transhumanism is now considered a growing field of study. Transhumanism has become a kind of cultural movement which shares postmodernism values (need for change, reevaluating knowledge...). It is close to philosophies of life and promotes the evolution of intelligent life beyond current human limitations by means of science and technology. In that way transhumanists call for improving the human conditions and ask scientists to find ways and means to achieve the elimination of ageing, enhance the intellectual, physical, and psychological capacities.

---

[1] *The Transhumanist Reader*, Max More and Natasha Vita-More, eds., Wiley-Blackwell, 2013.

A convenient approach to the aims of transhumanism can be found in *The Transhumanist Reader* by Max More and Natasha Vita-More.[2] Some 36 philosophers (very few of them can be identified as genuine scientists, even Ray Kurzweil cannot) exchanged their views on various topics about transhumanism. They do not claim to represent eternal truths but an evolving framework of attitudes for "continuously improving the human condition".

Transhumanism as a non-religious philosophy of life rejects conventional faiths, worship, or supernatural convictions. There are few Christians involved in transhumanist theories but much more Buddhists, whereas Judaists seem weakly reluctant.

Transhumanists refer to the French philosophers and dissenters of the Enlightment Century humanism. Their concerns quickly raise multiple issues around the nature and identity of the self. They consider that thinking or feelings are essentially physical processes; thus uploading minds to non-biological substrates is a straightforward conclusion to overcome limits imposed by our biological and genetic heritage. They also look to expand the range of possible future environments including space and virtual worlds.

The first fully developed framework (a handful of principles) of that philosophy has been defined in the "Principles of Extropy"[3] in 1990 later updated in 2003. As Max More puts it, "The Principles of Extropy do not specify particular beliefs, technologies, or policies. The Principles do not pretend to be a complete philosophy of life … The Principles of Extropy do consist of a handful of principles (or values or perspectives) that codify proactive, life-affirming and life-promoting ideals. Individuals who cannot comfortably adopt traditional value systems often find the Principles of Extropy useful as postulates to guide, inspire, and generate innovative thinking about existing and emerging fundamental personal, organizational, and social issues."

The word "extropia" has been chosen to show that transhumanists do not seek utopia but perpetual progresses toward an ever-distant goal to no longer suffer our current miseries. This is not a way to initiate predictions

---

[2] They are both deeply involved in the prospect of cryonics.
[3] Extropy Institute: http://www.extropy.org/

but more likely general expectations about technological advances without any idea about specific means or schedules.

Most of the transhumanists share the view that radical changes to the human condition will occur soon due to the scientific and technological progresses. Some forecast a Singularity to occur i.e. a one-time jump due to a burst in super-intelligence or in computing power. Others instead envision several steps modulated by economic or social conditions. All of that cannot be dissociated from a permanent consideration of risk inherent to uncontrolled changes.

Concerning the biological body, transhumanists consider it a piece of engineering (Richard Dawkins) and they seek to champion morphological freedom. This philosophy goes infinitely further than the current madness for tattoos, piercings, botox, sex changes, and other fancies. Debates rage about medical privacy, women's right to their bodies, and reproductive rights. In the face of the forthcoming changes we would need robust ethical principles to build on and a large dose of tolerance.[4]

A major concern of the transhumanists relies on the "life after biological death" and the possibility of transfer into a posthuman, virtual, synthetic, computational upload. There is a theory of "symbiogenesis" that is to say a conglomerate of life forms and not from a common ancestry (!).

In their view of the future relationship of man with machine some transhumanists convey a blurring of borders of body and technology as hybridized in the notion of Cyborgs in which "the human and the technological actually merge rather than merely being embodied" (Peter-Paul Verbeek). Current wearable technology devices help us to accommodate future changes and possibilities. Networks and abiding connectedness provide a new umbilical cord to exchange information between the external world and the bodies.

2. Transhumanism as an Organization?

So, if Transhumanism is not to be considered as a religion, would it be able to play an influence in the societies as an organization or a movement of thought?

---

[4]For a more extended discussion see Anders Sandberg in *The Transhumanist Reader*.

Up until lately religion represented values each one has (or is obliged) to share. That was the fundamental basis for established societies to get coherence and a common way of thinking. Religions were considered as a basic means of moral pressure and conviction on the individual to obey some form of common behavior. This power benefited some privileged who monopolized the institution: religious or state authorities wrangled to have the final say and make a purely material gain. This basic scheme has now been reproduced in various forms.

Today the lack of credibility of the religions induced by the way of life in modern societies has deeply deteriorated that situation of monopoly but the basic underlying working principle still remains valid and other forms of collective compulsion have arisen. The aim still remains the same: attract beliefs from deemed compelling elements, gather "adherents" around symbolic banners which have been psychologically locked. Then the movement becomes able to draw political conclusions with more or less hidden intents.

All of that currently expands on an international scale (as religions did and still do for some of them) under diverse shapes. Therefore the important thing remains to keep the "faith" through words and images in the media. This latent power is cultivated in adapted "masses" and used to serve causes which sometimes are weakly related to the initial pretext. These beliefs often rely on unverifiable or imaginary elements which are amplified and broadcasted by associated media to create a rumor that cannot be contested.

This allows generating an effective lever to have some influence in the political, economic, or strategic choices sometimes beyond the immediate will of the governments. A counteraction is hardly conceivable as long as a wide population follows the preacher. In this *modus operandi* we currently find many famous (non-governmental) organizations[5] such as the World Wild Fund, Amnesty International, Green Peace, IPCC, or other less organized but nonetheless efficient movements preaching for CO_2 elimina-

---

[5] It is worth mentioning that the well-known international organization Red Cross does not belong to the list and remains a purely technical organization to provide medical assistance in any case of catastrophes or wars where people have to be rescued. This is without any counterpart.

tion, climate warming, biodiversity, endangered species or, more important in the public opinion: the nuclear threat.

So, in such a diversified context, what could be stated about Transhumanism? It was told before that transhumanism is not a religion ... but ... that does not prevent transhumanists from treating it as one.

Aubrey de Grey is a major contributor to the transhumanist philosophy. He is an English gerontologist from the University of Cambridge and he headed a conference and entitled the "Christian Transhumanist Conference"[6] on August 25, 2018 held in Nashville, Tennessee, United States.[7] He is a longevity advocate who pleads against illness, hunger, oppression, injustice, and death. So large a spectrum!

3. Extended Longevity and Immortality

Methuselah was referred in the Bible as the undisputable winner in the longevity records at 969 years whereas Jacob (147 years) remains far behind! That legend has no real meaning nor any physical evidence. The recipe of such incredible longevities has never been revealed. To avoid such an uncertainty, men invented a reliable calendar and a corresponding recording of the important dates in a register.

Nevertheless, for millennia, men struggled to find some serendipity to challenge these marvelous performances ... unfortunately to date! The world champion for longevity (duly registered at 122 years) still remains Jeanne Calment. However, slowly but assuredly, with the improved healthy environment and collective soft living conditions we enjoy now, more people are getting closer and closer to the hundred years wall.

This was an evident sign of encouragement for the transhumanists who claimed that we could be able to strongly foster the process! More especially, there was a mythic limit[8] in the aging, that is to say the barrier of the 100 years. Nobody knows if such a limit is an intrinsic part of our very genetic constitution or if it is just a psychological fancy. Anyway, this was

---

[6] https://www.christiantranshumanism.org/
[7] https://www.christiantranshumanism.org/blog/2018-conference-announcement?fbclid= IwAR0b-LZxlWoZTuf2DfGvMFvUlqGii0Ihfn4QwqbBLaDLPKQdA01dfufVTy8
[8] Fillard, *Longevity*.

considered as similar to a wall quite difficult to overcome; recently Jan Vijq[9] asserted that a maximum attainable longevity was established at 125 years. As a matter of fact more and more centenarians are being recorded.

Transhumanists forecast that the huge population of researchers now at work all around the planet will eventually find solutions to rejuvenation, juvenescence, or even ageing reversal through modern biological means; these "improved" men would so reach a status of quasi-immortality.[10] Craig Venter is optimistic about the possibility of growing artificial organs from stem cell culture and 3D bio-printing giving rise to what he called a "bio-teleportation".[11]

This evolution in the life expectancy already in place (see Figure 4.1.) can be highlighted with the statistics and mathematical models, keeping in mind that statistics are worth giving collective conclusions to but are in no way an individual prediction.

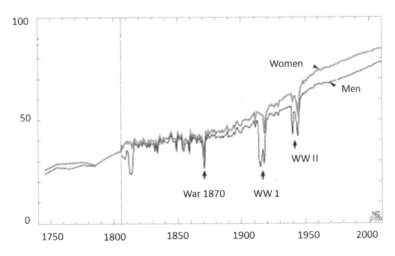

Figure 4.1. Evolution of the mean life in the past.

---

[9] *Aging of the Genome: The Dual Role of DNA in Life and Death*, Jan Vijq, Oxford University Press, March 29, 2007.

[10] *Au delà de nos limites biologiques, le secret de la longévité*, Miroslav Radman and Daniel Carton, Plon Ed., 2011.

[11] "Craig Venter's 'Digital-to-Biological Converter' is Real", Jordan Pearson, Vice, June 15, 2017. Available at: https://motherboard.vice.com/en_us/article/craig-venters-digital-to-biological-converter-is-real

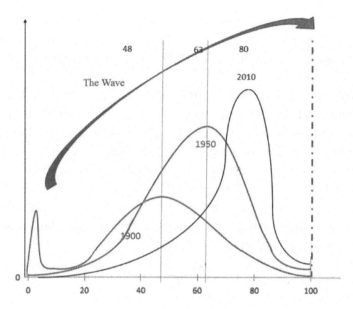

Figure 4.2. Evolution of the death profile with time.

In that way, it is observed that a calculation of the life expectancy, at a given epoch, and its evolution with the time elapsed, gives a reliable appraisal of the changes occurring in our destinies. Also the statistical profile of the death mean age and its distortion with time provide some meaningful information for the future to come (Figure 4.2).

Traditionally such a plot is to display a bell shaped curve (somewhat Gaussian if a pure random behavior is to be expected). These curves obviously change depending on the concerned population, from a society to another one, or even inside a same society depending on the social category considered. Each one belongs to its own statistics.

Surprisingly, we will observe that a large departure from this traditional behavior has occurred in the past decade and will likely develop as a more pronounced trend in the near future, coming closer and closer to the famous 100 years limit and prefiguring an overlap to come out soon. The "wave" of this evolution clearly appears on Figure 4.2. This likely next evolution is now even supported by the bankers[12] (which speaks for

---

[12] https://www.facebook.com/groups/longevity.alliance/?multi_permalinks=22482284285 97298&notif_id=1557545761141953&notif_t=group_activity

itself!): "One of the biggest investment opportunities over the next decade will be in companies working to delay human death, a market expected to be worth at least $600 billion by 2025, according to Bank of America analysts."

Obviously, such a current situation did not emerge from nothing. The 20th century had been an active period where key discoveries in medicine were to contribute to a longer and safer life: hygiene, surgery, vaccines or antibiotics, not to mention food, for instance, helped stamp out many terrible scourges such as small pox, typhus, cholera, tetanus, malaria, tuberculosis, and other plagues then deadly. This evolution is clearly highlighted in the statistics of the time. On top of that, we have currently entered a new age of medical instrumentation and body monitoring which contribute to a better appraisal of the issues coming.

All the signs are that a new civilization is ultimately to emerge, that could change our destinies as it is sketched in Fig. 4.3. Some more prophetic "transhumanists" even predict that, in a near future, we could commonly live until 150 or 200 years (we still have to wait more than a century to

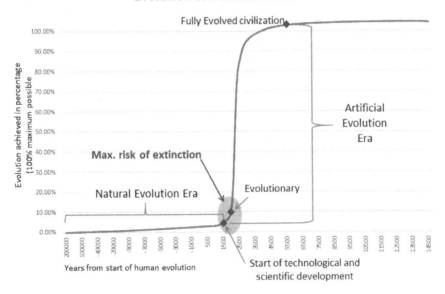

Figure 4.3. The near evolution as predicted by transhumanists.

know if these ultimate predictions are valid). This scheme is in perfect agreement with the Singularity thesis announced by Kurzweil.[13]

Such a widespread "rejuvenation" would induce lots of serious as well as unexpected social and economic issues to be solved, from the retirement age regulation and funding to finding a place for these newcomers in the active workforce, if they were able to contribute without overcrowding the job market. The tradeoff of these drawbacks would be the requirement for new jobs and new markets in healthcare or technology and overall economics; perhaps even a self-generating evolution of the employment opportunities.

All of that, also with the growing number of patients, will assuredly afford a much larger dimension for the science of gerontology which is to rejuvenate and soon become of key importance.

To make things more complex, geneticists have emphasized the need to draw up a plan to create purely artificial babies which could be "optimized" from the outset and immune against the most dangerous diseases or failures. They would also possibly be prepared as a machine to obey a "programmed obsolescence". Malthus might be right!

To complete the picture and to strengthen the hopes of the transhumanists it must also be said that immortality is not a fancy in our biological world of mortal creatures. There have been, throughout all eternity, some animals which are considered "quasi-immortals" such as the *Turritopsis Nutricula*. This jellyfish is able to endlessly regenerate its basic cells thus escaping the death process (except in the case of meeting an external predator). Such a mechanism can be run essentially due to the simplicity of the global organism; the same would be well more tricky dealing with a complex body such as in humans.

Following the likely near collapse of the 100 years wall, would the reign of Man slowly shift to a kind of reign of indestructible centenarians, thus inducing a new world order? Would there emerge a new age to replace the present basic Anthropocene? What could be the role of the Computer and the Robots in this new age?

Would this especially short period of Anthropocene be followed by an even shorter period we could name Robotcene? Would this be the

---

[13] Kurzweil, *Singularity*.

precursor to another drastic change where machines would have to play a decisive role? This is a little provocative but where are we heading to? Are we mastering the trajectory or is there a hidden will to prolong the evolution theory? Man had taken a long time to become "Homo sapiens"; now that he trusts to master everything, would he, all a sudden, turn into a "Homo Deus"?[14]

Now, the last "artifact" man invented (I mean the computer) is on the way to becoming even more "intelligent" and would soon challenge humans; that's a lot, because it (he?) is not doomed to die!

4. Brain Improvements and Super Intelligence

In the Stone Ages, millenaries ago, life was especially harsh for the primitive humans, who were, somewhat like animals. They were subject to common dangers (predators, wounds, diseases, famines, and so on). What made them different from animals was their ability to appreciate the surrounding reality[15] but, more important, the invention of language which helped them to speak and to think appropriately.

From these earliest times we got accustomed with more and more sophisticated "words" and we also got accustomed to use them to "think". It took time for such a "deep learning" to take place in our minds and stay organized. The brain is a very complex machine that is able, from the early times, to perform self-education and transmit its knowledge to the following generations as the acquired experience accumulated. Then a consciousness awakened and men began to take care of themselves.

As intelligence progressively grew, this resulted in a better knowledge of our environment and our own nature. This was a cumulative process which benefited everyone even if not everybody contributed. Intelligence applies to any domain of the human brain, not only to mathematics! So we now benefit from a huge thesaurus of what we call the universal "Knowledge" widespread in billions of brains and stored in external memories (the latest one being the Web) in order to be retrieved. Could we say this induced brain improvements along the centuries? Currently huge

---

[14] *Homo Deus*, Yuval Noah Harari, Harwill Secker London, 2015.
[15] Some would say intelligence.

efforts are made in view of a better appraisal of the brain functioning in order to enhance its performances.

This is a quite tricky job because a brain permanently changes with the interactions of memory, consciousness, and the subconscious (rather inaccessible). Also to be mentioned is the difficulty to rationally decide what is a "normal brain", an "exceptional brain" or a "perturbed" one. Then what remains to be improved and how? That question is not yet answered by transhumanists!

Cloning, graft, reconstruction of a brain have not yet been developed. However a partial graft of human neurons was attempted at a hospital in Rouen (France) whereas attempts to fix a brain (of a mouse!) using embryonic cells mutated into neuronal ones was also satisfactorily (?) performed experimentally in Belgium. As of now we must be satisfied with the first success of a reversed ageing process obtained on human cells.[16] An Italian surgeon has bluntly emphasized grafting a whole brain on another body, but is that really possible? At the moment, there is no way to noticeably improve human intelligence biologically so we turn to … computer which is constantly improving!

5. Digital Life

As far as transhumanism is concerned, data and algorithms are changing our life; the awareness of importance of the digital 2.0 world leads to understanding the innovations and their impact on our minds and relationship between us. This also conveys the risk of a possible technological alienation.

5.1. *Information or disinformation?*

Digital communication[17] makes possible an instantaneous flow in the digital channels close to the forms of speech (rapid but imperfect) even if

---

[16] "Ageing in human cells successfully reversed in lab", Lorna Harries and Matt Whiteman, *The Conversation*, August 10, 2018. Available at: https://theconversation.com/ageing-in-human-cells-successfully-reversed-in-the-lab-101214

[17] *The Digital and the Real World*, Klaus Mainzer, World Scientific, 2018.

written as short messages. Instead of the vanishing sound these messages are able to remain in the memories of the devices for years or forever.

Some call[18] the fluctuating mass of these correspondents a kind of digital "swarm" made up of isolated individuals! These digital swarms express an ephemeral and very apparent power.

From a pessimistic point of view these channels also convey more and more fake news (unconscious or intentional) as long as they play the role only of passive transmitters of signals without verification or critical analysis actions. As Talia puts it "A large mass of individuals contribute to the post-truth era, digital neo-proletarians of an informational massification that weakens cultural and civic values and subtracts meaning to information sharing." Hopefully he moderates his rhetoric: "Alongside this multitude of replicating transmitters, there is however a much smaller set of original producers of information, opinions, and analysis. These subjects consciously use digital communication as a new and original form of expression".

Facebook gathers data from anywhere it can and is spying on everyone to get better business deals whereas innocent people (some 1.5 billion connected people every day) live in their own bubble.[19] Texting has replaced conversation for many children, phone addiction has gotten commonplace and a growing percentage of children prefer virtual experience to the real world. It is worth taking a moment to reflect on the profound changes we have seen in just a generation following the entrance of the digital world.

There are mounting fears about the impact of AI and facial recognition. This last point has the potential to threaten individual privacy to the very letter, revealing your instant state of mind or mood according to the correlated voice recognition. With neuroscientists getting better at accessing brains would some people be able to enhance their mind with a chip, so making them smarter? This scary idea belongs to the transhumanist's theories.

Now people track their health using their smartphone, smart watch, keyboards, and screens. This leads to a kind of depersonalization of the

---

[18] *Big Data and the Computable Society*, Domenico Talia, World Scientific, 2019.

[19] "How to fix social media before it's too late", Roger McNamee, *Time*, January 29, 2019.

relationship with their doctor whereas privacy and security of the data are challenged.[20] Nevertheless AI already provides considerable help in diagnosing cancer, diabetes, and many other diseases.

5.2. *The society of the future*

Within the last decades our societies have already changed and they will still change a lot more soon. The previous behavior was rather static but the new world of easy exchanges, communications, job requirements, tourism development, and professional competition has upset the traditional habits and opened up unexpected behaviors.

Information is now everywhere with the media, the social networks, Google, and the Internet of Things (IoT). Nothing can be concealed from Big Brother, not even our private rooms, and it's going to get worse in the future.

People have entered into the practice of readily changing jobs or even profession, to fly to the other side of the planet to follow or search for a professional opportunity and in such a context it becomes therefore a serious headache to preserve a quiet work-life balance. Both husband and wife are subjected to such constraints of mobility to the point that many are reluctant to start a family. Having a dependent child has become a real burden. This situation has generated deep issues in China for instance (or Japan as well) where girls are less numerous than boys and are very much concerned with their future professional lives.

On the other hand, Chinese couples have to take into account that, when having reached the retirement age they will become dependent on their children (preferably boys). So they are not reluctant to consider the benefits of generating the "best optimized" child they can, perhaps through germinal enhancement. Would not parents in Western countries soon feel the same way?

There are deep changes to be expected in the social organization of the immediate future where a slowdown in the global population growth could be expected in spite of the steady extension of the life expectancy for elders[21] and even if many populations in the developing world do not

---

[20] "Deep learning", Eric Topol, *Time*, March 25, 2019.

[21] And also with the uncontrolled birth rate in the undeveloped countries.

undergo these recent constraints and still largely and irresponsibly procreate as animals do.

All of that has led us to wonder how robots could play a role in the sexual equilibrium of the populations. Sex dolls are commonplace in Japan but currently the same is developed for women and it appears that they become more well appreciated since AI makes them able to speak and actively participate in chatting (this is a very important point concerning women!). Robots might well be expected to become acknowledged sexual partners[22] after a while.

So it is no longer a daydream for transhumanists to imagine a world where robots participate in our daily intimate life whereas babies will be artificially grown and biologically "enhanced". Embryo breeding is now well mastered until a week of "culture", the limitation being only a matter of international moral conventions. At the same time the gynecologists and obstetricians are able to save premature babies only 22 weeks with a consistent rate of success. The 21 weeks gap between these two limits only remains a technical adjustment for an artificial incubator able to follow the size evolution and needs of the embryo, as it is spontaneously performed in a natural womb.

Artificial spermatozoids have already been created from scratch and they resulted in 2009 to normal mouse pups after growing in vitro. The corresponding ovocytes were of natural origin but researchers pledge to soon obtain artificial ones. This means that artificial motherless (and fatherless too!) babies are for tomorrow (at least for mice!).

This raises some futuristic questions: are we heading now to unacceptable transgressions of the basic moral laws? Does the "natural" procreation yet become essential? Would an artificial social organization be required to take its place? Who'll decide?

In the wake of such a new universe, if the onset of puberty was to be cancelled, would so the ageing process be stopped and at what stage? What would the future transhuman look like where God is no longer of any help?

---

[22] "Mostly Human" by Laurie Segall. Available at: https://money.cnn.com/mostly-human/i-love-you-bot/

6. Would Transhumanism be a Kind of Russian Puppet?

Transhumanism carries scattered ideas corresponding to virtual worlds where altered forms of consciousness expand opportunities for experiences and escape the conventional system of moral constraints. The future becomes a world of "avatars" where an individual thereby becomes a multiplex or protean personality.[23]

As William Bainbridge puts it: "Transhumanists philosophers have suggested varied viewpoints of simulation, consciousness, or existence and they notably argued whether humans could or do reside within a simulation."[24] Whereas Thomas theorem states that: "If men define situations as real, they are real in their consequences".[25]

In that situation the enhancement of human abilities is part of the virtual world of Avatars. This will be addressed in future operations of teleoperation of personal robots. The notion of embodiment plays an increasingly prominent role in philosophy and cognitive science. A "profoundly embodied" robot is so engineered as to be able to learn to make use of a variety of external sources of orders. They are forever testing the possibility of incorporating new resources and renegotiating their own limits.

The human "self", then, emerges as rather a soft one straddling the boundaries of biology and the artifact (robot). However this hybridization is not without raising spectra of subjugation and monstering.

Transhumanists, as explained by Max More, are no longer only involved in philosophical discussion as they have now shifted emphasis to implementation. The previous Precautionary Principle, as an absolute principle, calls for restrictive measures so leading to a paradox which would stop all progress. However the Proactionary Principle appears as a type of model for dealing with change and structuring decision-making when possible. As More says "the underlying Principle is less like a sound bite than a set of nested Chinese boxes or Russian babushka dolls",

[23] "Transavatars", William S Bainbridge in *The Transhumanist Reader*.
[24] "Simulation, consciousness, existence", Hans Moravec. Available at: http://www.frc. ri.cmu.edu/hpm/project.archive/general.articles/1998/SimConEx98.html
[25] *The Child in America*, William Thomas and Dorothy Thomas, A Knopf New York, 1929.

keeping into account the diversity of the situations and making response and restitution proportionate.

To complete the picture of a robot embodied in a brain Moravec suggested an experiment he called "Brain in a vat" that merges the reciprocal situation of an isolated brain put in a vat and connected to a multiservice robot to play the role of the body. This organization would allow recording the orders and possibly replacing, bit after bit, the personality and thought of the brain which becomes clearer and clearer to the machine. This would be a direct way to download a mind into a machine. Up to now, this remains a pure imaginative fancy as long as a deprivation of sensory and the "bodylessness" will inevitably lead the mind to hallucinate!

In order to hallucinate a little more, it is worth concluding this chapter with a discussion about the delirium of the philosophers. Throughout all eternity they were irresistibly attracted by the indecipherable mysteries of our existence: the "self", the death, the soul (eternal?), and so on. Theories, predictions, models abound giving rise or following religious convictions.

Now that scientific investigation begins to shed some light on the behavior of this strange organ (the brain), philosophers are boosted to imagine new frontiers without any limit. Transhumanism welcomes these initiatives even if they could be contradictory or without any positive support.

Most of them reflect an essential idea of personal identity even in the context of a radical cognitive enhancement. God's involvement in the immortal soul seems not to be essential to explain the "self" (John Locke). He also argued that the self "is an illusion created by the contiguity of sense perception and thoughts" whereas Thomas Metzinger thinks that "the neuroscience shows that the 'self-y' feeling is simply a useful heuristic that our minds create, without any underlying reality".

Concerning the "Engineering transcendence", Giancarlo Prisco dares to say that "science may someday develop the capability to resurrect the dead" and "proposed to base a transhumanist religion on this idea". He considers that mind uploading is the "Holy Grail" of transhumanism. That would make us free of our biological brains and grow beyond limits! Such an uploading could be performed through a destructive scanning of the biological tissue or preferably (!) a non-destructive one even if experts disagree on a possible timeline.

However such audacious thinkers still go further. They imagine that, someday it will be possible to gather information from the past and so make "time travels" as archeologists do currently. This is often called "Quantum Archeology"! After death "we may wake up in a simulated environment" as featured by most religions! If we are living now in a simulation, that could be a logical consequence.

Hopefully Giancarlo Prisco agrees that "I am the first to admit that this is a mythology and not a scientific theory." And, to conclude, Robert Geraci proposes that "Apocalyptic AI" is a religion based on science without deities and supernatural phenomena.

The problem remains that if, somewhere in the world, basic morale or religious convictions lead to refute inadmissible ideas there will always be a place somewhere else where they will be accepted and implemented without restriction. We are now at the point where it becomes possible to soon transform ourselves into something "other" (see Gregory Stock in *The Transhumanist Reader*) whatever it could be.

Part II
Possible Pledges

Chapter Five

Present Achievements and Transhumanism

Transhumanism was for a long time an extension of the imagination of thinkers as a future for humanity. More recently, modern science and technologies have given stronger support and push for the dreams of nonscientific people to justify their conclusions. Then the previsionists, who rely on the new discoveries of scientific experts, arrived and engaged in extrapolations justified on real elements. Obviously there is no limit for the imagination and we must be cautious not to jump hastily to definitive conclusions about post-human beings.

In this chapter we will look at the philosophers who tackle the problem and also how science and technology have provided them with food for thought.

It is worth observing that the disciplines which previously enjoyed rather little interference (medicine, chemistry, physics, or biology) and used to work independently, now have become closely tight and, to some extent, interdependent due to the use of modern digital instruments.

1. Transhumanism, A Matter for Philosophers

Without going into the *Epic of Gilgamesh* or even Pic de la Mirandole, the philosopher Friedrich Nietzsche[1] can be considered an influence on the

---

[1] *Nietzsche: Thus Spoke Zarathustra*, Robert Pippin, ed., Cambridge University Press, 2006.

birth of transhumanism philosophy with his prophecies of the "Death of God" and the "Übermensch". Max More,[2] for instance, drew his ideas from Nietzsche. The first idea of transhumanism might have been proposed by JBS Haldane,[3] a British biologist ahead of his time. He was motivated by a search to create and sustain life with artificial means to improve human health or intelligence, which idea will become a basic transhumanist theme.

Then came Julian Huxley who is considered the founder of the current transhumanism and invented this term in 1957. He said, "The human species can, if it wishes, transcend itself — not just sporadically, an individual here in one way, an individual there in another way, but in its entirety, as humanity."

Huxley describes transhumanism in these terms: "we can justifiably hold the belief that these lands of possibility exist, and that the present limitations and miserable frustrations of our existence could be in large measure surmounted..." The idea of a technological Singularity has been proposed initially by Irving John Good in 1965.

Then the first meeting of the followers took place in California in 1990 at the University of California Los Angeles (UCLA) which had become the main center of transhumanist thought in 1980. A local TV (EZTV) proposed a lecture ("Third Way") with Natasha Vita-More who helped to advertise the event which transformed into a worldwide transhumanist movement.

Later in 1998, philosophers Nick Boström and David Pearce founded the World Transhumanist Association (WTA) to promote transhumanism as a legitimate subject of public interest. The proposed formal definition was:

1. The intellectual and cultural movement that affirms the possibility and desirability of fundamentally improving the human condition through applied reason, especially by developing and making widely available technologies to eliminate ageing and to greatly enhance human intellectual, physical, and psychological capacities.

---

[2] *Transhumanism: Towards a Futurist Philosophy*, Max More, 1990. Available at: https://web.archive.org/web/20051029125153/http://www.maxmore.com/transhum.htm.

[3] *Daedalus or Science and the Future*, J B S Haldane, Cambridge, 1923.

2. The study of the ramifications, promises, and potential dangers of technologies that will enable us to overcome fundamental human limitations, and the related study of the ethical matters involved in developing and using such technologies.

Later WTA transformed into "Humanity+" which claims to be "the future vision of a new intelligent species, into which humanity will evolve and eventually will supplement or supersede it."

Transhumanist philosophers argue that it is possible and desirable for humanity to enter a transhuman phase of existence in which humans enhance themselves beyond what is naturally human. In such a phase, natural evolution would be replaced with deliberate participatory or directed evolution.[4]

This was not without questioning old convictions including religions. Some thinkers were driven to adopt a firm atheist conclusion[5] for the immediate future and claim there is no longer room for God, whereas others[6] still defend established religious traditions.

Over the succeeding decades the boost was given by Ray Kurzweil,[7] soon followed by Hans Moravec, who swung between technics and previsionist speculations. Since that time Kurzweil (now with Google) has become the indisputable "guru" of the transhumanist philosophy. Then the conceptualization of Transhumanity or even Posthumanity was developed by Ran Ettinger[8] (a mathematician convinced "cryonics" militant). Max More[9] as a philosopher founded the "Extropy Institute" and gave his definition of transhumanism:

"Transhumanism is a class of philosophies that seeks to guide us towards a posthuman condition. Transhumanism shares many elements of humanism, including a respect for reason and science, a commitment to progress, and a valuing of human (or transhuman) existence in this life."

---

[4] https://humanityplus.org/philosophy/

[5] *The God Delusion*, Richard Dawkins, Black Swan, Penguin UK, 2006.

[6] *God's Undertaker*, John C Lennox, Lion Books, 2007.

[7] *The Age of Spiritual Machines*, Ray Kurzweil, Penguin Books, 2000; Kurzweil, *Singularity*.

[8] *Man into Superman*, Ran Etttinger, Avon, 1974.

[9] See above note 2.

Artificial Intelligence and cognitive enhancement are the most favorite themes for the transhumanists. In their imagination these technical achievable goals could lead to a new species of Man and at the same time conduct to find technical solutions to enhance life expectancy. This last point is actually a current trend already noticeable to the extent that Kurzweil did not hesitate to foresee a limit to occur soon in the range of 150–200 years (not to say 1,000 years!) as soon as the biological means for rejuvenation or age reversal will be implemented.

This biological evolution looks to be challenged by the machine in a tight competition as announced by Marvin Minsky[10] (computer scientist) as soon as 1960.

1.1. *Contradictory opinions*

Such a bold theory as transhumanism brought together a large variety of thinkers from pure philosophers to qualified scientists but that has not taken place without generating strong objection from many others who did not trust in the prediction or were afraid of the possible threatening drawbacks.[11] Many prominent transhumanist advocates refer to transhumanism's critics on the political right and left jointly, as "bioconservatives" or "bioluddites". A belief of counter-transhumanism is that transhumanism can cause unfair human enhancement in many areas of life, but specifically on the social plane.

The most vehement opponent to transhumanism forecasts might be Francis Fukuyama[12] a political economy professor at Johns Hopkins University in the U.S. He is followed by other bio conservators such as

---

[10] "Steps toward Artificial Intelligence", Marvin Minsky, 1960. Available at: http://web.media.mit.edu/~minsky/papers/steps.html

[11] See for example, "Transhumanistes contre bioconservateurs", Jean-Michel Besnier, February 25, 2016. Available at: https://sciences-critiques.fr/transhumanistes-contre-bioconservateurs/

[12] *The End of History and the Last Man*, Francis Fukuyama, Free Press, 1992; Our Posthuman Future, Francis Fukuyama, Farrar Strauss and Giroux, NY, 2002; *La confiance et la puissance*, Francis Fukuyama, Plon, 1997.

Jean-Michel Besnier,[13] Wesley Smith,[14] Jeremy Rifkin,[15] or Bill McKibben.[16] The fear is that the advanced technologies could harm our human dignity or erode something fundamentally precious (religious convictions or secular motivations).

They claim that the best counteraction might be to implement drastic and global bans for the enhancement of technologies implying human values which could lead to a posthuman degraded condition.[17]

In 1989 Fukuyama published his first essay[18] "The End of History" where he argues that humanity had reached "an end point of mankind's ideological evolution"; that was essentially motivated by the end of the Cold War which generated a wave of political changes and Fukuyama's celebration of the rise of "liberal democracy". This is properly quite marginal with respect to transhumanism but nevertheless constitutes a background of his philosophy.

One of the main criticism by the anti-transhumanists is to accuse the transhumanists of "playing God". The Vatican, in 2004, stated that "[c] hanging the genetical identity of a human person … is radically immoral".

In 2001 a Center for Genetics and Society was created which expressed a radical break with possible human cloning. For their part George Annas and Lori Andrews[19] warn of practices in violation of Human Rights: euthanasia, segregation, genocide of inferiors. They definitively reject a wild research of performance at the expense of men being left behind: Cyborgs+ against Minus.

2. Science and Technological Contribution

Transhumanist thinkers study the potential benefits and corresponding dangers of emerging technologies that could overcome fundamental

---

[13] *Les robots font ils l'amour?*, Laurent Alexandre and Jean-Michel Besnier, Dunod, 2018.

[14] *Culture of Death*, Wesley Smith, Encounter Books, London, 2000.

[15] *The Emerging Order,* Jeremy Rifkin and Ted Howard, G.P. Putnam's Sons, New York, 1979.

[16] *The End of Nature*, Bill McKibben, Anchor, 1989.

[17] Transhumanisme et Intelligence Artificielle, Nick Boström. Available at: https://iatranshumanisme.com/transhumanisme/transhumanistes-vs-bioconservateurs/

[18] "The end of history", F Fukuyama, *The National Interest,* 16, 3–18, 1989.

[19] In *War Against the Weak: Eugenic Campaign to Create a Master Race*, Edwin Black, Four Walls Eight Windows, New York, 2003.

human limitations as well as the ethical consequences resulting from the use of such technologies. For instance the roboticist Hans Moravec has deeply influenced transhumanism[20] and post-humanism by rethinking the relationships between humans and increasingly sophisticated machines.

As Irving John Good puts it: "there would then unquestionably be an 'intelligence explosion' and the intelligence of man would be left far behind. Thus the first ultra-intelligent machine is the last invention that man need ever make".[21]

Marvin Minsky, for his part, was a "cognitive scientist" involved in the AI research at MIT; he tried to make a bridge between philosophy and the technical world. He was a pioneer[22] in artificial neuronal networks and was at the origin of a strong controversy. Some claim (his book) to have had great importance in discouraging research of neural networks in the 1970s, contributing to the so-called "AI winter".[23]

As a matter of fact the progresses in computer science have made a large contribution in the evolution of the physical means now open in every domain, but the most important application may lie in the biological field which largely benefitted from these facilities to open new perspectives at the molecular, cellular, and even body level.

Molecular biology is at the crossroads of physics, biochemistry, and genetics and aims at discovering the general role of cells in the life mechanisms. For a long time people believed that the living was governed by the laws of chemistry but that these laws were different from those of inanimate matter. Now we understand that the basic laws are the same and that no vital force breathes life into matter as suggested by religions and vitalist theories.

The main contribution was the discovery of the DNA molecule and its recent decoding of the hidden information (James Watson, Francis Crick and finally Craig Venter). That made it eventually possible to

---

[20] "When will computer hardware match the human brain?", Hans Moravec, *Journal of Evolution and Technology*, 1, 2006.

[21] "Speculations concerning the first ultraintelligent machine", Irving John Good, *Advances in Computers*, 6, 31–88, 1965.

[22] *Perceptrons*, Marvin Minsky and Seymour Papert, MIT Press, 1969.

[23] "A sociological study of the official history of the perceptrons controversy", Mikel Olazaran, *Social Studies of Science*, 26(3), 611–659, 1996.

modify this molecule using the technic of CRIPSR cas9 (molecular scissors of Emmanuelle Charpentier and Jennifer Doudna at California University) and fix genetic mutations. This played directly into the arms of the transhumanists, who jumped to the conclusion that changing (enhancing) Man was for tomorrow.

That discovery of our intimate being also raises the possibility of substantially lengthening the useful life (Miroslav Radman[24]) so rekindling the enthusiasm of every transhumanists who see there a tremendous source of hope. Ray Kurzweil (and followers too) promised an extended life span in the range of 150 or 200 years.

Even if such eventuality could look a bit crazy, that does not prevent daring researchers from trying to do the impossible in spite of widespread international criticism. In November 2018, Jiankui He, a Chinese biophysics researcher at Shenzhen University claimed that he had created the first human "genetically edited" babies, twin girls known by their pseudonyms, Lulu and Nana were reportedly born on 8 November 2018. He justifies this bold initiative by the fact that the father of the girls was seropositive and claimed he has accordingly modified his genome using the CRISPR technique. It would appear thereafter that both babies are well but Jiankui would have been fired from his university and gone off the radar!

With neuroscientists getting better at accessing brains and altering thinking, we are reaching a world where we could also change our mind. That again belongs to the very realm of transhumanism.

What changes now with science and consequently technology is the new dimension given to research and development efforts. We have become more sensitive to changes because of the new potentialities that have arisen, some of which were previously considered as in the realm of God's will or science fiction! We have to face new challenges even if no definitive answer appears. How far will we go too far?

Would Science be able to replace the idea of God in human minds (at least some of them) and change it drastically? Would the simple idea of God be sustained in the young generations who are more devoted to their smartphones!? Would *The Singularity is Near* be considered as the new

---

[24] *Au-delà de Nos Limites Biologiques*, Miroslav Radman, Plon, 2011.

Bible?[25] From time immemorial, long before the arrival of the 2.0 world, Man has confronted a major challenge: to counteract the natural order.

We are experiencing situations so far unthinkable where it would be feasible to artificially create a man from scratch in an "improved" version. The Pre-Implantation Diagnostic (PID) allows to sort the "good" embryo among a collection, to be implanted through In Vitro Fertilization (IVF). This is an accepted form of eugenics that would allow to create little brother with the sole aim to make a compatible bone marrow donor for his leukemic older brother. It remains very difficult to condemn such a decision. Such a genetical lottery is bound to give only winners!

3. The Electronics Revolution

To uncover the origin of modern sciences we must turn towards the history of electronics that started a century ago. This new science launched a new era for the whole humanity. The influence of the corresponding discoveries can be compared, without exaggeration, to that of the discovery of mastering fire some millennia ago. Transhumanism theories are nothing more than a philosophical consequence of the social changes induced by the various technologies that followed the birth of this new science of electronics.

The story started with Thomas Edison who discovered that a carbon filament was able to provide light if electrically heated; he then put the filament in a glass bulb to protect it and that was the first light bulb which was to replace previous light sources (candles or petrol lamps).

In the wake of the light bulb, some researchers (like Frederick Guthrie in 1873) discovered that heated metals were able to emit electrical charges (electrons) and Edison used this property to make the "vacuum" electrically conductive between an emitting filament and a metal plate positively biased. This phenomenon was called "Edison effect" further explained and put into equation by Owen Richardson (Nobel Prize 1929). That story lead to the first "vacuum diode" that was used by John A Fleming in 1904 to detect radio waves. That was the first electronic "tube" (or "lamp" or "valve") later improved to give birth (Lee de Forest) to a long series of

---

[25] See note 7.

more complex lamps dedicated to more sophisticated functions of detection, amplification, and modulation of the electronic signal. The new science of electronics was born.

The applications soon followed, namely with radio transmission which changed the world by making long distance instant relations possible for the first time in history, a large leap from the Morse invention of telegraphy. Voice, image, and later video communication became feasible.

It is also worth mentioning that these discoveries in the "free electron" behavior also led to a side branch which later became of key importance: the discovery of X-rays[26] by Wilhelm Röntgen in 1895. More recently this discovery coupled to a digital facility gave rise to the famous Computer Assisted Tomography (CAT or scanner) that revolutionized the art of medicine by giving the first three-dimensional real time imaging of the interior of the human body. This epoch was indisputably very rich in new perspectives, a real, astonishing firework that announced the arrival of an explosive future. Transhumanists were especially shy, as they did not dare to imagine such a revolution to come!

Then, electrons became the center of a wide curiosity for the scientists who wondered how these electrons were "living" inside the matter, more especially in these materials they called "semi-conductors" which can conduct electricity or behave as insulators depending of the external circumstances (temperature, light, bias, ...).

Then the crucial event arrived: the unexpected discovery of the "transistor effect". Three researchers at Bell Labs (William Shockley, John Bardeen, and Walter Brattain) discovered in 1947 that it was possible to regulate the displacement of electrons inside a little bar of Germanium crystal, from an external command. They were later honored with a Nobel Prize.

Their experiment gave rise ten years later[27] (!) to the first radio receiver equipped with "solid state devices". These new components were to advantageously replace the previous cumbersome and calorigenic vacuum lamps; they were the size of a moth and equipped with three "legs" as shown in Figure 5.1 and the material used has become Silicon.

---

[26] So dubbed because of the mysterious nature of that new radiation at the moment!

[27] There tends to be a delay between a scientific discovery and the development of an operating industrial application.

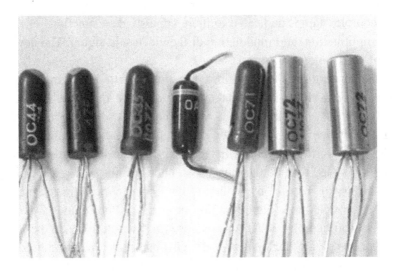

Figure 5.1. The first transistors.

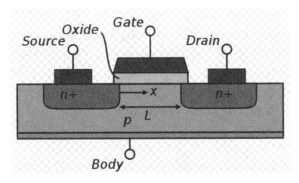

Figure 5.2. Field effect transistor (FET).

Progress was noticeable but also encouraging. Further improvements came with a new version of the transistor: the "field effect transistor" (MOSFET or MESFET) which relies on the surface of the sample instead of the bulk, as shown in Figure 5.2 and works like an electronic tap.

The fabrication of this version was improved using implantation technics and an automated production of the circuits which allows the fabrication of thousands of circuits in a same operation. The size of the achieved transistors now lies in a micronic range and researchers struggle to reach the still smaller quantum range with "Qbits". This induced the explosion of a fantastic realm of new instruments which were to definitively change our lives: telecommunications, scanners, satellites, 3D printers, super-microscopes, Nuclear Resonance Imaging, Data Centers, smartphones and, of course ... the essential computers! Then transhumanists awakened and philosophers will marvel!

The FET system was rather simple and works as an interrupter: on / off depending on the gate polarity. This was at the origin of the digital world which functions with electrical pulses (bits) and obeys the mathematical binary algebra invented long ago by George Boole[28] in 1840 and rehabilitated by Claude Shannon (see[29] for more details).

These small components have now invaded our daily environment and multiplied by billions. They have become so small that they can no longer be seen as well as the microbes, but that does not mean they are not there. Computers were born and spread in our daily environment and became our life partners. It is enough, now, to look around to see people talking into their smartphones or playing a game in any circumstance. This addiction clearly supports the predictions of the transhumanists that we are driven to intimately collaborate with machines. The smartphone, the connected objects, the self-driving cars, as well as the credit cards are just the very beginning of what awaits us soon.

Memories also benefitted these crowding Integrated Circuits (ICs) to the point that data centers began to increasingly hoard information about any subject and AI has become required to dig in that mess to safely "search and retrieve" the data.

In the wake of the transistor also flourished photo cells, light emitting diodes (LED) and flat screens which allowed mastering the pixels of the images in a high resolution way. As a result of image manipulation, the confidence people had on the valuable testimony of an image is vanishing as we are now flooded with images real or doctored to the point that discriminating between information and disinformation has become a real issue.

---

[28] *The Mathematical Analysis of Logic*, George Boole, 1847.
[29] https://en.wikipedia.org/wiki/Boolean_algebra

With this tool at our disposal it has become possible to implement plenty of devices which lead to the sophisticated instruments capable of obeying algorithms and finally promoting an AI. This is, in short, the fabulous destiny of the electrons to serve humanity as loyal slaves. It only remains to appreciate the fair value of that collaboration.

3.1. *The instrumentation*

Among the multitude of dedicated instruments that the digital world has generated special mention must be given to those devoted to the "sequencing" of RNA / DNA molecules. These molecules were initially discovered by Friedrich Miescher in 1869 before falling into oblivion because proteins, rather than DNA, were thought to be of superior interest.[30] The situation drastically changed in 1953 when crystallographers James Watson and Francis Crick put forward their double helix model of DNA using adapted X-Ray technics, each strand being composed of four canonical bases of nucleotides referred to as A, C, G, and T.

This endless molecule was considered very difficult to analyze, but in 1995 Craig Venter (a newcomer) succeeded, for the first time, in sequencing the complete genome of a bacteria before doing the same thing with human brain cells. His approach was systematic and focused on complementary DNA broken random fragments the results of which are later reassembled in a computer. The work of Venter generated many controversies but it was unquestionably the origin of the current instrumentation which mixes biological and computer technics. This initial work took ten years and more than a million dollars from the National Institutes of Health.

Today, sequencing techniques have become mandatory for basic biological research and in numerous fields such as molecular biology, medical diagnostics, biotechnology, virology. The instruments have become fast and cheap as, for instance, the Shotgun Sequencer of Craig Venter. Other competing methods are under study which relies on atomic force microscopy (AFM) or transmission electron microscopy or even electron tunnel effect. The raw data so generated need to be

---

[30] At that time the opinion was that proteins hold the genetic blueprint to life.

assembled and this operation needs to overcome many computational bioinformatical challenges.

As all of these machines become more widespread, there come new issues about storage, security, and sharing of data. Ethical issues have also been raised by genetic variation screening (newborns as well as adults) to detect future diseases.

This new universe of the intimacy of the body has been of a key interest for the transhumanists who see there the future way to change the human being toward a more promising future.

3.2. The computers

The story of the computer[31] began with analog computers using punchcards produced by IBM and used in the Manhattan Project to make the first atomic bomb. They already demonstrated (in spite of frequent breakdowns) that the machine was faster than any hand-operator. Enrico Fermi eventually found that the world of digital computing was worth exploring and in 1946 the first programmable computer ENIAC was built for the Army. The machine was built around a huge collection of Vacuum Lamps (or Valves). The story goes that they were too many lamps so there were rumors that there will always be some of them out of duty and the "computer will never get to the end of job"! That did not prevent Edward Teller from using the machine in his early work on nuclear fusion reactions!

The arrival of the transistors strongly encouraged IBM to propose more powerful and more secure second generation digital machines and the word "Computer" became commonplace. These computers associate a "processing element"[32] and some form of memory. They are assisted by peripheral devices which help communicate two-way with the machine. The next step came with the advent of the Integrated Circuits[33] and the invention of the microprocessor (Intel 4004) on a microchip.

---

[31] "On computable numbers with an application to the Entscheidungsproblem", Alan Turing, *Proc. London Math. Soc.*, 1937.

[32] Central Processing Unit (CPU).

[33] Jack Kilby (at Texas Instruments) and Robert Noyce (at Fairchild Semiconductors) in 1958.

Computers have been originally used (since the 1950!) to coordinate information between multiple locations but now computer networks resulted in the well-known World Wide Web (Internet) and satellite relays. The future is shared between possible optical computers, DNA computers, neural computers, or quantum computers; the sky is the limit!

The role of the computer is to solve problems the way it is programmed but Artificial Intelligence and Machine Learning now makes it possible to learn and adapt the conclusions in an "intelligent" way. For transhumanists who aim at imitating the human brain and push for extended performance by the machine, this is their cup of tea.

The historic start[34] of the race for Supercomputers was given by Seymour Cray (CDC 6600) in the 1960s and from then on it never slowed down. The arrival of the Big Data facilities and Internet vigorously boosted this vicious circle. The game unit universally accepted to rank the super machines is no longer the MIPS but now the FLOPS[35] and there is a fierce competition globally to reach the top record of the fastest machine.[36]

The first work of such computers, of course, is to "crunch" the mountain of raw data recorded and stored in huge memories, to select the relevant ones and put them in the right order before entering a program of "intelligent" interpretation. All of that, not to mention the many endeavors to "digitalize the world" as Google puts it or to "understand", simulate, and possibly copy the human brain as IBM entices it with its Blue Gene/P which aims to simulate 1% of a human cortex or a complete rat's brain (not yet achieved)!

4. Neurosciences and Brain Exploration

Cognitive neurosciences are concerned with the biological processes underlying cognition and mental processes. The many branches of this

---

[34] This was quite heroic because the transistors at the time were individual bipolar germanium devices. Today this looks rather simplistic and prehistorical!

[35] Million Instructions Per Second (MIPS); FLoating point Operations Per Second (FLOPS).

[36] Currently the Blue Ribbon belongs to "Tianhe-2" (China) with 33.86 Peta Flops ($33.86.10^{12}$ operations per second).

field rely on psychology, neurobiology, and computational modeling; we are close to brain exploration and computer modeling. A new class of supercomputers has emerged which tends to reproduce the behavior of the human brain but without directly copying the biological neuron. They are called Cognitive Computers and they combine AI with machine learning algorithms. A specific microchip called True North was developed by IBM.

These "smart cognitive systems" infer and in some way think well beyond the limits of the basic preconfigured computing rules and aim at reaching operating speeds in the range of the PetaFLOPs[37] with massively parallel architectures. Some had said a 100% human-like scale simulation (estimated to require 4 Petabytes of memory) should be achieved by 2018 (but it was not the case). Brain Research through Advancing Innovative Neurotechnologies (BRAIN) was a collaborative "moon shot initiative" launched by Barak Obama in 2013. This effort is at the same amount of financing that previously was the White House Neuroscience Initiative which already initiated the Human Genome Project (HGP) in 2003. However as Yann LeCun[38] puts it "while Deep Learning gets an inspiration from biology, it's very far from what a brain actually does".

Singularity, as presented by Kurzweil appears as a point where man and machine are to merge in new concepts and new beings. Biology is to be reprogrammed, mortality will be transcendented, ageing will be mastered with new nano-technologies, red cells will be replaced by more performing nanorobots, brain will be interfaced with computers, AI will make super human intelligence possible including the possibility to make a back-up of the mind (in case of what?). That is the Kurzweil future world.

Barak Obama would have said: "We are able to see the galaxies or very little things like the atoms but we still have a lot of mystery with these three pounds of nervous tissue between our ears". R.U. Sirius[39]

---

[37] FLoting Operations.

[38] Yann LeCun is the (French born) AI director at Facebook. He remains famous for publicly warning his counterpart Ray Kurzweil at Google, for an excessive media hype ("too much to be honest" he dared say!).

[39] *Transcendence*, R U Sirius and Jay Cornell, Disinformation Books, 2015.

(Ken Goffman) wisely uses this word "Hardmeat" to refer to the (soft) biological "hard" which backs the brain activity in opposition with "Softmeat". To make a copy of a brain requires deciphering in the depth of how it works, i.e. the soft part, and that is not for tomorrow. The complexity and upgradability of this bio-electronic structure may not be so readily fully understood; thus, making a software copy of it is not so obvious despite what Kurzweil said of it, who foresees such a completion within the next five or ten years at the most for a "transcendent man".[40]

Such projects[41] for identifying the wiring scheme (or "connectome") of the brain have been flourishing for years around the world following different approaches. Some are trying to recognize and record the paths in a living brain by means of high resolution MRIf[42] providing microscopical scale views; others are more interested in the functional and structural links, at a macroscopical scale, between the cortical areas and structures.

Several projects for understanding the brain functioning are currently ongoing: Blue Print for Neuroscience Research or Big Brain (NIH), Whole Brain Emulation (Univ. Lausanne, Swiss), Blue Brain, or Human Brain Project (Europe) for instance, not to mention similar organizations in Japan or China. All of that induces huge funding from the corresponding organizations and transhumanists are eager to get results which could support their philosophy. Incidentally, I noted from a press release[43] that an Italian neurosurgeon (Dr Sergio Canavero), in a research group from Torino, proposes to make a complete head transplant and is looking for "donors"! That should assuredly be a culmination!

Currently we do have very sophisticated and effective means to begin to get information about the way the brain operates, even with the help of detailed three-dimensional digital images (thanks to the computer!). The electroencephalogram (EEG) assisted by AI allows a better understanding by correlating the signals recorded simultaneously from many probes

---

[40] In *The Singularity is Near*.

[41] *Brain vs Computer*, Jean Pierre Fillard, World Scientific, 2017.

[42] Magnetic Resonance Imaging (functional). High resolution is obtained by increasing the magnetic field (currently 4 to 11 Tesla in the latest equipments).

[43] "Le neurochirurgien qui veut transplanter une tête humaine en appellee à Bill Gates", *Midi Libre*, June 13, 2015. Available at: http://www.midilibre.fr/2015/06/13/le-neurochirurgien-qui-veut-transplanter-une-tete-humaine-en-appelle-a-bill-gates,1174702.php

stuck at different places on the skull. It is often used in conjunction with other means of analysis (CAT, PET scan, MRI, etc.) to reveal correlations and remove ambiguities.

These new opportunities open the door for exchanging real time information with machines even if the direct way back, outside/inside the brain is not truly available but requires vocal assistance.

Also to be mentioned is Computer Assisted Tomography (CAT) which gives impressive 3D images and also the fantastic MRI which also gives 3D images specifically of biological species of molecules of biological parts such as, for example, blood hemoglobin which is a main tracer of the brain's local activity. The improvements obtained for such MRI apparatuses currently allows to get voluminous images in a quasi-real time, thus making it possible to follow in detail blood circulation in the brain. This is the basis of what is called the "functional" MRI or MRIf which makes possible a real video of the brain activity.

All of that means may be used to tentatively (but vainly up to now) explain the most hidden behavior of the brain that remains hard to imitate by a computer: the transcendence. For the phenomenologist (and the philosopher), the transcendence is "what transports our consciousness above our objective perception, beyond any possibility of knowledge".

Transhumanists refer to everything which confirms or surpasses the concept of the technological Singularity to come. They pretend that "there will come a time when the technology will be able to progress by itself in its own elaboration and its complexification; humans will then adopt an attitude of confidence and surrender toward the self-sustained technological progress". Would the human-like computer have to address this domain and include a module of transcendence and its more dedicated extension, the religion? This is a very special point that is worth an extensive discussion (see previous Chapter) but Kurzweil warns us: "if I was asked if God exist, I would say 'not yet'", adding "God like powers". But others commented: "will we be the gods? Will we be the family of pets? Or will we be ants that get stepped on?"

Chapter Six

Information, Communication, and Artificial Intelligence

As soon as Man developed upright posture and some neurological changes, he benefited from a great leap in cognitive ability with the possibility of reaching the abstraction domain. Then complex thoughts were exchanged and accumulated knowledge transmitted from a generation to the following one. This obeys a circular scheme — as shown in Figure 6.1. As time passed the speed of flow accelerated and machines began to contribute to speeding up the process, thus leading to faster communications (Space), larger memories (Data Bases), and so improved knowledge that AI was required to dig in. This is the mechanism the transhumanists propose to explain the fast changes due to the technological improvements and consequences.

The question now is whether AI would be limited to finding information in a huge stack of data (search engine) or if AI would be able to play a larger and more intuitive role similar to a genuine human intelligence (as long as we can get a realistic definition of it). The answer is mixed, even if transhumanists are convinced that, with time, the computer will inevitably win and be a direct competitor.

Frank Chen announces that "this is deep learning Cambrian" to mean that a new age is coming for AI, whereas Andrew Ng (Baidu) adds "AI is the new electricity, just as 100 years ago electricity transformed industry after industry, AI will do the same" and Jeff Dean (Google Brain Project)

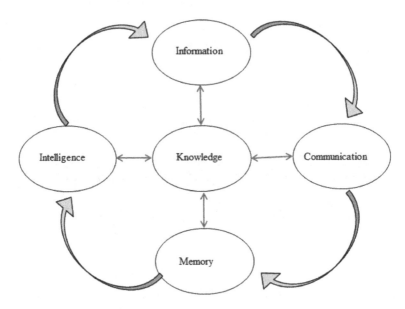

Figure 6.1.   The information flow.

considers "that computers have opened their eyes".[1] What an avalanche of promises! But, up to now, if computers cannot reason, that might just be coming soon. All these quotes are to bring to light the large scale involvement of so many relevant scientists in the rocketing field of AI.

1. Where Does Intelligence Come From?

Usually one says that Intelligence might be the proper province of the human being even if there could be some doubt about this statement. In any case, this ability considerably varies from a brain to another. It is in no way a gift of Nature (or God!) but the result of an accumulated knowledge from millenaries and transmitted through education, teaching, experience, and practical training. Intelligence is forcibly a result of a collective process even if it belongs to an individual acquiring. To give an exact definition of intelligence remains a major and subtle challenge.

---

[1] "Andrew Ng says Deep learning is the 'New Electricity'; what this means to your organization", Jeremy Howard, fast.ai, October 11, 2016. Available at: https://www.fast.ai/2016/10/11/fortune/

The biological neuronal organization of the brain does not obey a standard but a diversified model which makes the collective behavior of the neurons richer. The challenge is open with the computer which draws its power from its extensible memory able to accumulate everything without sorting what could be of a future utility and the useless remaining (what the brain does instinctively). There is still a deep mystery in the way the brain operates whereas the computer is a clear construction of Man which mystery only relies on ignorance.

A question then arises: how to confidently characterize and measure this immaterial intelligence. An empirical solution was elaborated on the basis of a standard questionnaire: the test for Intelligence Quotient (IQ). Obviously this standard operation hardly fits with the largely diversified shapes of human intelligence. Be that as it may, the test cannot take into account the whole diversity of minds. To improve the IQ it was found that, statistically speaking, the environment and education could play a decisive role (so-called Flynn effect).

This effect has been noted at the world level: some say that the average IQ scores would have increased dramatically over the last century as the world has learned better ways to think and to teach. This is quite amazing when we look around us!

This has been used by Chinese researchers encouraged by a permissive government to justify their research; they succeeded in doping the DNA of mice in utero and found the mice became more intelligent! A transfer of the technique to monkeys is on the way and why not on humans in the future as foreseen by transhumanists? Stem cells are also promising candidates for such a selection.[2]

There is no denying that IQ has a dark side, as emphasized by Galton. IQ could be an effective tool to carry out screening for survival in case of an excessive population threatened by hunger in a Malthusian politic.

Intelligence is required in mathematics or any other scientific culture but intelligence also helps to face unexpected situations and find the most suitable solution. This last occurrence remains the most formidable task for a computer even equipped with an advanced AI. At the moment, this obstacle is the focus of the transhumanists' attention.

---

[2] "Embryo selection for cognitive enhancement", Carl Shulman and Nick Boström, *Global Policy*, 5(1), 85–92, 2014.

Some unexpected situations often surge, all a sudden, over a person's life and require an immediate answer and action. This was the case for the pilot of the plane that was affected by a reactor failure just after taking off from New York's La Guardia airport. He instantly and instinctively reacted and crashed the plane straight ahead in the Hudson River, thus saving the lives of all the passengers and crew. This is a typical example of a reaction a computer would not have been able to provide.

Man is an autonomous being who alone decides his fate. Transhumanists strongly support this idea of the right to self-determination; more especially everything is allowed to control disease or ageing even using dedicated brain memory implants; this is a key point in their "religion". In this domain they recognize the ultimate prominence of the human over the computer (even if the computer may efficiently contribute to finding adapted cures and diagnostics).

So the question remains: where does the Cyborg begin? Many artificial organs (digital as well as biological ones) are already available or on the way to being experimented. High hopes were invested in a possible artificial heart; trials were not yet effective but this is the price to pay for such a man/machine revolution.

At the state level there is already a global super-intelligence race; some transhumanists are convinced that this could lead to a sort of domination for the first nation able to complete a fully conscious super-AI computer.

2. What Does Information Mean?

Information is a word that physicists invented (as well as the term "Energy")[3] to qualify a virtual notion related to knowledge, memory, intelligence, communication. From that on, the main importance of being able to isolate and quantify this abstract notion comes with the immediate necessity to give it physical support able to make it possible to transfer the content elsewhere. This notion of information is inseparable from that of communication. Information is a volatile notion the only usefulness of which relies on transmission, through an inevitable coding process.

---

[3] Energy is a notation intended to describe and quantify a fugitive exchange occurring in a physical, chemical, biological reaction or transformation. This is purely virtual; nobody has ever seen a kWh nor a Calorie, only their relative effects.

When a brain elaborates a particular piece of "information" out of its unconsciousness and sends it to consciousness, it immediately codes it with the words he has learned. We used to have words to think! Then it relies on an emitter (vocal chords) to create a "signal" (acoustic voice) which is able to propagate and reach a remote detector (ear) which reconverts the signal (sound) into an exploitable medium (nervous flow or electrical converter) and reaches the detector (brain of the correspondent) where it is decoded and possibly understood.

This universal organization of the information transfer follows, from time immemorial to the 2.0 world of digital satellites, under various forms but always the same scheme, as indicated in Figure 6.2. The transmission delay could be brief or very long depending on the situation.

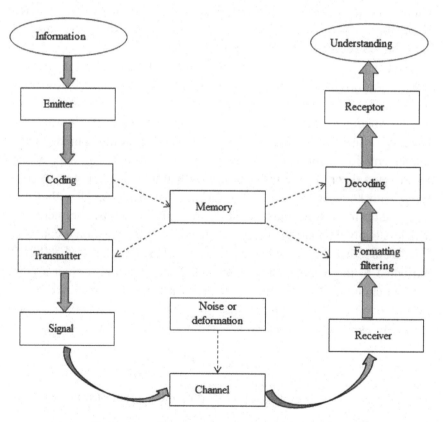

Figure 6.2. Organization of information transfer.

When Cro-Magnon painted his hand on the wall of his cave he might have thought, calling to a future fictional visitor "Hey Joe! This is my hand, you know!"; he might have forgotten it but the message was sent. Several millennial later a certain Joe discovered the painting, understood the coded information and hopefully this Joe said "Hi Bill! I have found your painting! This was your hand I guess! The same as mine! Good Lord!".

This is a funny example of long range transfer of information. Today, we send spacecrafts in the deep space faraway to play exactly the same game of communication, hoping there would be, somewhere, an "Alien-Joe" to receive it and understand the meaning of such information. In the remote times of the Cro-Magnon world there were possibly some transhumanist-like people equally anxious to imagine a future for this humanity which had just discovered how to make fire and, perhaps, also worried about the possible consequences of this astonishing discovery and the alarming power it gave to the "master of fire".

But what do we intend with this word "information"? Information theory[4] was originally elaborated by Claude Shannon and Norbert Wiener in 1948. The aims of it were: the evaluation of the source information and the information capacity of a channel, also the coding of the information in order to fit with the channel requirements. This was required for the implementation of modern long range communication. The crux of the information theory is the measure of information which is not to be confused with knowledge or meaning and also intimately implies that this information to be transmitted is not previously known by the receiver.[5] The less likely the message the more precious the information it conveys. That means that the information measure is based on the probability P attributed to the element to be transmitted (at the limit through a pure random choice). That also means that the measure is in no way directly related to the meaning of the information. Then the mathematical formulation, in a standard convention, is expressed by the formula:

$$I = \log_2 1/P.$$

---

[4] See *Communication Systems*, 3rd Ed., Bruce Carlson, McGraw-Hill International Edition, 1986.

[5] In such a case the information is of no value and does not need to be transmitted.

And the corresponding unit (following John Wilder Tukey) is the "bit" (for binary unit).[6] This definition holds for analogic messages as well as digital ones.

Why did I say "digital"? This point will be developed further but this is to differentiate from what is called analogic. Classically, a message — such as arising from voice or a microphone or otherwise — consists in a continuously varying parameter (sound pressure or electrical voltage or else). As it is, this message can be distorted or polluted by an additive perturbation (noise) coming from the surrounding. This "pollution" will not be easily isolated from the message (filtering).

On the contrary the digital message is obtained by partitioning the analogic signal into individual samples[7] which can be transmitted as they are or their value can be individually coded (yes or no digits coding in bits). Then the message is secured because the code can proceed from a repetition of the coded sample information thus improving its security.

In the past, not so far from now, information encountered difficulties to be shared. The language skills were reserved for educated people who could speak Latin in order not to be understood by less-educated people. Information thus was a precious commodity to be preserved. The means for dissemination were limited (books) and slow even if based on long term transmission. This situation was often closely guarded by the scholars. Things have changed with modern times and the widespread democratization when instruction has been largely developed in order to provide any citizen with the ability to read and write.[8] Previous social inequalities have soon become unsustainable in our modern minds. At present, the Web has further enlarged this ease at which anybody can get any required information in a jiffy, regardless the nature of this information.

Some transhumanists claim[9] that education and schools have to go a step further to make information even more open to the young. It is claimed that teachers have to integrate digital techniques to teach and even

---

[6] Not to be confused with the "bit" or "binit" (binary digit) used in the digital language.

[7] The Shannon-Hartley theorem tells that the sampling frequency must be more than twice the maximum bandwidth of the analogic message.

[8] The famous three Rs of the basic instruction broadly granted: reading, writing and arithmetic.

[9] *La Guerre des Intelligences*, Laurent Alexandre, JC Lattès, 2017.

personalize their teaching methods with the help of neuroscience and genetics based on a better appraisal of the scientific workings of the brain. Such a brain power upswing will be necessary in the competition to come with machines. Such a "neuro-augmentation" should become essential to enable us to handle the amount of information to manage.

3. Communication Systems

Coding information to send far away is in no way a 2.0 novelty! For a long time peoples all over the planet used to send agreed "smoke signals" to announce important news. Then the Chappe telegraph[10] was invented allowing a longer transmission of more detailed alphabetic visual messages. But modern communication systems started off with the prophetic phrase by Samuel FB Morse in 1838: "Attention the universe, by kingdom right wheels!".

Thus was born a new era of electro-magnetic (radio) as well as optical communication (optical fiber). Over the next nearly two centuries communication engineering has advanced to the point that text, data, voice, images have become integral parts of modern life, through space facilities and down the oceans, all over the planet. The occurrence of AI created a strong stimulation in the communication systems to manage the huge fluxes of transfers and make linkage easier.

The space technology also contributed to induce a new dimension of communication links, to the point that satellites now convey a permanent flux between computers (Internet or else) and correspondents. Everybody handles a smartphone and billions of words continuously pour across global networks, thanks to these systems. There is now a full and continuous relation between people wherever they are. This is a provisional form of global brain connection which shall develop in the future. The sky is the limit!

Even robots now require communicating between them to exchange their data. Skynet is already active but a dedicated space network is under implementation that will be devoted to machines (RoboEarth) and using a specific language such that they could also benefit from similar facilities

---

[10]This telegraph is historically famous to have transmitted what is called "the Ems dispatch" which quickly triggered the 1970 Franco-German war.

(RoboBrain) on the cloud to exchange, in a less informal way, their experiences through AI or human collaboration thus sharing algorithms and learnings. All of this clearly prophesizes the coming of an autonomous machine era envisaged by the transhumanists.

Communication systems as they are, up to now, were only meant to transmit the message as faithfully as possible and in an impersonal way. With the increasing power of computers and the abundance of communications, such a limitation could appear dated. The sophisticated technology of AI allows to keep an eye on the content of the message in order to verify if it does not contain unwanted elements (drug traffic information, political disclosure or disinformation, and so on). More especially social networks like Facebook became at the forefront of current events for this reason. This is inherent with the fact that they are of a large use from the simple individual to the high level politicians and contribute to the global debate. Of course, this intrusion also implies some drawbacks such as the facility for infringing the basic freedom of expression which is a fundamental universal right. This is no longer a science or technology issue but only an equilibrium to reach in the way we use them.

4. How to Use Information?

In the Middle Ages the painted cathedrals played a persuasive educative role. People from the country did not usually have the opportunity to see images and they considered these artworks as a direct emanation of the divine; so they were strongly induced to follow the simple messages they carried: have a better social behavior, trust in God and you will access Paradise or on the contrary be sent to Hell and burn for eternity. The message was simple but very convincing. Such images at that time were rare but had a strong persuasive power, as intended by the clerics.

This conviction that the images are a testimony of reality was largely admitted. When photography was discovered the photographic prints were considered as indisputable clues of reality, even if some photographers were gifted in making fakes. Today that is over. We are flooded with images and we have become very skeptical about the truth they could convey. The computer has opened new horizons with the possibility to "paint" any image we could want, even in a video format which associates with movement in order to be more convincing. Images bring us to the virtual world and information has turned into disinformation with fake news. How to get through this mess? What is to be trusted in?

The coming generation of humans are now making a difference from the previous ones, showing a strong individualism extended to the whole society and a marked passion for virtuality as they can find in their omnipresent machines. Noreen Herzfeld is afraid of this drive towards violence: "The prevalence of violent video games among teenage boys where one can play in 'The God mode' and control life and death. Playing violent video games may be rewriting the human brain or at least enhancing those brain centers associated with violence and aggressive behavior."[11] We have come so far since the days of the painted cathedrals!

Information, in general, is now abundantly available by means of communication systems and databases. The Internet has become so common that a majority use it daily and the knowledge therein largely accessible in great detail. I remember the times in the past when accessing information in scientific reviews was a heavy, slow, and hard track that now comes with a click of the mouse!

There was a time when even photocopy did not exist! I often feel I was born in the Middle Ages, some half a century ago! This personal observation fairly supports the transhumanism theory of the immanent acceleration of the things. This change in the facilities to reach information was really a decisive step to accelerate the pace of scientific research and make it more efficient. It could very well be the case that only people of a certain age are sensitive enough and able to feel this evolution, whereas the younger generation are already accustomed to it and find the 2.0 world quite "normal" as if this was the state of things all along.

5. Artificial Intelligence

As we are not able to cover such a wide subject in a few pages, let us only focus on the important issues that are concerned with transhumanism. We have tried to split the matter into dedicated sections but an overlap or

---

[11] *Technology and Religion: Remaining Human in a Co-created World*, Noreen Herzfeld, Templeton Press, 2009.

repetition in the material has been inevitable. Artificial Intelligence has stimulated a large number of authors some of whom have been referred to in this section, or directly cited.

Artificial Intelligence is not a new revolution even if the current results are really amazing. Things began with the advent of mechanical automation equipment, the first of which was due to James Watt who as a young assistant had to manually regulate a vapor machine with a throttle. The story goes that he was quickly bored by this job and got the idea to link with a string the throttle lever to the turning balls indicating the speed of the machine. Then the "automated" machine was allowed to self-regulate its operation. The machine then became in some way "intelligent", even if in a very simplistic manner.

Textbooks define AI as "the study and design of intelligent agents"[12] where intelligent agent refers to a system that perceives its environment and takes actions that maximize its chances of success.[13] AI research is divided into many subfields but General Intelligence is among the field's long term goals. After many highs and lows, AI has today become an essential part of the technology industry and contributes to the most challenging issues in computer science.

Computers have become so good at deciphering writings (even manual) that it there was a need to invent a way to stop their inquisitiveness; thus CAPTCHAs were proposed to block them:[14] Completely Automated Public Turing test to tell Computers and Humans Apart. In this way the letters are so distorted and disorderly arranged that even an "intelligent" computer cannot read them (but the humans could!).

5.1. *China, the first Singularity?*

"Singularity" is a word that can be broadly interpreted in various senses. It could for example describe quite well the recent explosion of the

---

[12] *Computational Intelligence: A Logical Approach*, David Poole, Alan Mackworth, and Randy Goebel, Oxford University Press, 1998.

[13] "Artificial Intelligence", Wikipedia. Available at: https://en.wikipedia.org/wiki/ Artificial_intelligence

[14] "The changing science of machine learning", Pat Langley, *Machine Learning*, 82(3), 275–279, 2011.

Chinese economy which has now reached a top level global position. This could assist as a first version of what transhumanists are waiting for.

In a few years China has evolved from a global workshop of low cost products into a high tech champion in every domain: biology, computers, space, smartphones, and even ... Artificial Intelligence. Concerning the latter topic this new Super-Power is implementing an impressive social post-modernity organization which could be somewhat a model for a transhumanist future. Huge data centers have been grown which are able to house a collection of extended personal data, at the size of the country, and this is not for fun but for keeping a tight individual control on the behavior of each one. Facial recognition and AI are extensively unfolded; nothing escapes the attention of the camera network.

Still more impressive, the smartphone company Huawei succeeded in developing the first 5G generation of smartphones which some, outside China, already consider as an indecipherable spy to thrive all over the world and bring back information. Would all of that anticipate a foreseeable post-Singularity order for a future post-human organization, for the best and the worst?

Chinese researchers have no taboos and are keen to explore new horizons as soon as they look accessible. Modified embryos have been, for the first time, fully developed in China in spite of a widespread moral reprobation. These researchers will likely soon take the lead in this field.

Nevertheless there are serious threats in the evolution of this continent-sized nation. The recent changes in individual prosperity transformed a typically peasant population into an essentially urban society with the corresponding basic demands. These changes induced a profound evolution in the Chinese demeanor, especially with the rising expansion of the senior population concomitant with a drastic reduction in the births. This induces lots of issues which hamper the occurrence of a "steady Singularity". No doubt that computers and AI are to play a key role in bringing solutions.

Economic issues have appeared with the 4-2-1 structure of Chinese families; this means that an individual citizen who has a job must take care of his two parents who may not have retired with money enough for living expenses as well as the four grandparents who have nothing to live on.

That also means that this guy does not wish to make a baby! Young women in China are less numerous than the male population, they are somewhat reluctant to get married and often are busy with their jobs which would influence their decision to have a baby.

These issues will urgently require decisions on how to allow the seniors to recover or recycle their skills to allow them to contribute and earn their living for as long as possible. This problem is in no way limited to China and has begun to be seriously tackled in every developed country. In this domain AI will certainly be of some help if a specific adaptation is implemented. China is expected to enter a recession as soon as 2029. No wonder there is already a rich/poor gap due to deep social inequalities.

AI techniques are already on probation in several social contexts in many countries in order, for instance to take care of employees in especially dangerous jobs and provide them with an "e-guardian angel", to bring people assistance in their professional life or pamper the nervous or physical fatigue. This is quite comforting but the counterpart is to extend such a policy to also emphasize control of the behavior of every citizen through a system of notation of their social behavior in any domain and this is quite disturbing as suggested by transhumanists! AI can then bring to a dictatorial power either a human despot ... or a machine.

5.2. *What about AI?*

The possibility of an AI universally compatible with human intelligence is currently irrelevant even if extensive researches make significant progress. At the moment expert systems are the only way to implement an efficient AI (but limited to a specific relevant field) which can accordingly challenge human intelligence in the specified domain. As Boström puts it, "Rule based programs that made simple inferences from a knowledge base of fact, which had been elicited from human domain experts and painstakingly hand coded in a formal language." This is purely GOFAI (Good Old Fashioned AI).

The cleverness of such expert systems becomes more and more relevant even if it also becomes more and more uneasy to follow the track of the algorithms embedded in the black box. Yet it remains essential for the human to keep a hand on the real fit of the system with the matter in question. Obsolescence of knowledge is valid for the machine as well as the humans.

Humans have been, for a long time, able to learn from experience but machines now also have access to this ability through neural networks. Machines have become able to implement learning processes[15] allowing more refined approaches such as generalization, correlation, and hidden statistics. Multilayered neural networks make it possible to execute massively parallel sub-symbolic processing or connexionism (as used in the genetics' programs). Such disparate techniques can be successfully assembled: "decision-trees", "logistic decision models", "naive Bayes",[16] etc.

These software techniques were especially efficient in the AI for game competitions. In some way we became accustomed after the bright victories of the machines in Chess, Go and even the famous Jeopardy! Nilsson[17] relativizes these successes: "AI has by now succeeded in doing essentially everything that requires 'thinking' but has failed to do most of what people and animals do 'without thinking' — that somehow is much larger".

Today AI tackles still more elaborate problems such as pattern recognition (face, voice, texts...), theorem-proving or equation solving; they are by now so well established that they are hardly regarded as AI anymore. Larger AI fields also move further and drive the software science for Internet social networks and e-mail correspondence surveillance not to mention autonomous military robots. However this excessive confidence in the AI sometimes leads to catastrophic breakdowns such as the crash of the world stock market in 2010.

Nevertheless this does not prevent extrapolation of new paths for a Super AI to be implemented: brain emulation, biological cognition, human-machine interface and network structures.

---

[15] "Learning representation by back-propagating errors", David E. Rumelhard, Geoffrey E. Hinton, and Ronald J. Williams, *Nature*, 323, 533–536, 1986.

[16] *Machine Learning: A Probabilistic Perspective*, Keven P. Murphy, Cambridge MIT Press, 2012.

[17] *The Quest for Artificial Intelligence*, Nils J. Nilsson, Cambridge University Press, 2009.

5.3. *Deep learning and back propagation*

Huge data centers have now accumulated a tremendous amount of information which requires adapted means to "search and retrieve" specific elements. Special algorithms were implemented to boost the deep neural networks.

The goal of such algorithms is to find a function that best maps a set of inputs to an estimated correct output. This is extrapolated from the way a neuron works. The information is presented in a layered structure and the inputs provided with a "weight" even if set randomly; the discrepancy between the actual output is compared with the expected one. The first layer is devoted to determining a key feature of the input by intuiting complex features of the words and identifying them. Then an optimization process is implemented to minimize the error. More details can be found in a recent paper of Le Cun[18] who has become a champion of the technique!

Unsupervised learning is the ability to find patterns in a stream of input. Supervised learning includes classification and numerical regression. Reinforcement learning rewards good responses and punishes bad ones in order to form a strategy.

The first success was rather strange! The machine (16,000 microprocessors) was sent an access to YouTube and asked to say what interesting and repetitive things are to be seen in the videos proposed, without any more requirements. The proposed video files were all displaying various cats in different situations and the machine, on its own, recognized that the interest should be on a particular "object" which can be identified in all the videos despite its changing aspect and which corresponds to what we know as cats. Dean said "it basically invented the concept of cats!". What was left was for the machine to know that the name of the "object" was "cat" and it will never forget what a cat resembles! This was a breakthrough, a first step in the knowledge; but it still remains that the machine ignores how a cat behaves and what a cat really is. There comes the issue of consciousness. Google has now started building brains of its own instead of hiring human brains! All of this demonstrates that brain like

---

[18] "Deep learning", Yann LeCun, Yoshua Bengio, and Geoffrey Hinton, *Nature*, 521, 436–444, 2015.

machines can be emulated without requiring copying a brain, strictly speaking. However this shows that, progressively, the initial target of a search engine evolved into a larger and more intelligent machine to copy the way a human would search.

Jeff Hawkins and Andrew Ng speculated that the brain may have also one fundamental algorithm for intelligence which could play a similar "deep learning" in the cortical column. This could be in accordance with the well-known "plasticity" of the brain. The idea is supported also by Yudkovsky: "Humans have around four times the brain volume of chimpanzees, but the difference between us is probably most brain-level algorithms".

Another way to get to an improved AI could be to build a "seed AI" that would self-improve intelligence following the same way a toddler or a child proceeds.[19]

5.4. *Cyborgs and humanoids*

Thinking is the essential role of the brain but a larger activity relies on the management of the body and corresponding sensors in order to allow the human to face the permanent constraints of the environment in the unforeseeable situations life is bringing. The challenge between the brain and the computer is not restricted to thinking but more essentially to action. This research is mainly performed in the U.S.

Humanoid or "animal-like" robots[20,21] were especially designed to work for rescue operations in disasters or hazardous areas such as, typically, the Fukushima nuclear plant. They have to be optimized for mobility, dexterity, strength, and endurance. They, *a priori*, are not intended to physically resemble a man (or a woman!), only functionality is important. However this human simulation quickly meets its limitations. For instance it is well much easier to make a driverless car (that is quite a done deal) than to make an android driver which would have to learn how to get in the

---

[19] "Computing machinery and intelligence", Alan Turing, *Mind*, 49, 433–460, 1950.
[20] "Iron man", Lev Grossman, *Time*, June 8, 2015.
[21] The dog-like robot "Spot" was developed by Boston Dynamics and is able to perform many delicate missions in the military as well as civilian domain.

car, reach the wheel and the pedals … and also get out, which happens to be the more complex operation! The car has been made for a man, not a Cyborg nor a full machine, and the man does the job so simply and quickly! Even though such a "machine" has recently successfully passed the test. The only problem was that it took a tremendously long while to perform this whole operation, a man would have done it in a jiffy!

Human beings solve most of their problems using fast intuitive judgments rather than the conscious step by step deduction that early AI was able to model. AI has made some progress at imitating this kind of "sub-symbolic" problem solving; neural nets attempt to simulate the structures inside the brain that give rise to this skill and statistical approaches mimic the human ability to guess.

Han Moravec, Kevin Warwick, and Ray Kurzweil have predicted that humans and machines will merge in the future into cyborgs that are more capable and powerful than either. Here we come close to science fiction: Luke Muehlhauser[22] reports that the idea of intelligence explosion once machines can start improving themselves is the basis behind many of the intelligence-explosion arguments. For his part Hajime Sorayama's depiction of sexy robots in an actual organic human form the "Gynoids"[23] is an unnatural product of the human mind, whereas Edward Fredkin and George Dyson[24] argue that "AI is the next stage in evolution".

Meanwhile sophisticated applications are mainly carried out in Japan with different intents. Many Androids are already taking the place of a hostess at the reception desk of a museum such as Kodomoroid and Otonaroid which welcome you at the Mitsukoshi exhibition in Tokyo. They are able to answer questions in various languages. The resemblance is really uncanny! This innovation is quite impressive but still far from being confused with a human even though the evolution is fantastically fast.

To get closer to reality the android must be trained to analyze the facial expression in a video signal and real time; this new kind of software

---

[22] *Facing the Intelligence Explosion*, Luke Muehlhauser, Kindle Edition MIRI, 2013.

[23] *"The Gynoids,"* Hajime Sorayama, Nippon Shuppan Hanbi; GMBH, 1993.

[24] *Darwin Among the Machines*, George Dyson, Basic Books (US), 1997.

is under study in France[25] to get information on the interlocutor (man, woman, age, humor, emotions, sight direction, speak recognition on the lips …). The second step for the Android, following the feelings related to the environment, would be to control the aspect of its own face in correspondence with the situation. The robot is also not yet able to create artificial vocal cords; the voice of the Android comes out of an ordinary loudspeaker. To get a better human resemblance, Japanese developers are trying to synchronously distort the lips of the manikin following the phonetics of the language.

Intuitive approaches are also developing to extend generic AI methodology:[26]

• Apply templates of deontological rules to the situation.
• Present the AI with massive databases of moral evaluations of situations given various predictive features.
• Generative modeling of humans and how their cognition works.
• Reinforcement learning and modeling human psychology.
• Inverse reinforcement learning to learn the reward function and then port it into AI.
• Cognitive science of empathy to be better understood and could be engineered into AI.

5.5. *The threats induced by AI*

Microtargeting machines begin to learn on their own and "weaponize" AI. A company already hoovers up mountains of consumer personal and lifestyle data in order to reach a "psychographic" profile of you and be able to push your "emotional buttons". This is worse than a religion; this is a rational machine, precise, personal and fast. Cambridge Analytica (UK) claims to have gathered detailed profiles of 250 million Americans and this company is not the only one in the business. Then it has become possible

---

[25] Among many well reputed companies (Google , Facebook and others) a start-up is to be mentioned: SmartMeUp company located in Grenoble.

[26] "Thoughts on Robots, AI, and Intelligent explosion", Brian Thomasik, 2014. Available at: https://foundational-research.org/artificial-intelligence-and-its-implications-for-future-suffering/thoughts-on-robots-ai-and-intelligent-explosion-2/

to direct the minds of individuals in an optimized way and persuasively suggest particular actions such as buying a washing machine or even ... vote Macron! This automated psychological drive could be as efficient as the "idea of God" to induce controlled behaviors. These machines have the benefit of certain autonomy; they are now able to manage their own content, evolve, and make decisions on the fly. The computer is on the way to becoming a direct challenger of God.[27] Purely "intellectual AI" is on the way. Collective human intelligence will certainly be seriously boosted by the machine. Such a symbiosis is suggested by Joël de Rosnay who asked a bizarre question: "would the computer get moral and be uncompromising as some religious could be (or have been)"?[28]

Here are some comments, opinions, and corresponding fears expressed by popular transhumanists:

Boström's book[29] has, in places, the air of theology: great edifices of theory built on a tiny foundation of data. It's all too easy to develop elaborate mathematical theories around imaginary entities. AI is vastly more efficient than a human brain; also it might be vastly larger because it hasn't had millions of years of evolution to optimize its efficiency.

Han Moravec and Ray Kurzweil have argued that it is technologically feasible to copy the brain directly into hardware and software, and that simulation will be essentially identical to the original.[30]

Stephen Hawking, Bill Gates, and Elon Musk have express concerns about the possibility that AI could evolve to the point that humans could not control it, with Hawking theorizing that this could "spell the end of the human race".[31]

Martin Ford argues that AI applications in automation will "ultimately result in significant unemployment as machines begin to match and exceed the capability of workers to perform most routine and repetitive jobs. As a matter of fact this could be considered short-sighted, as other

---

[27] "AI's killer app? Duh ... marketing", Dan Lyons, *Fortune*, March 28, 2017.

[28] *Je cherche à comprendre*, Joël de Rosnay, Les liens qui libèrent (LLL Ed.), 2016.

[29] *Super Intelligence*, Nick Boström, Oxford Press, 2014.

[30] "Logic and probability", Lorenz Demey, Barteld Kooi, and Joshua Sack, Stanford Encyclopedia of Philosophy, 2013.

[31] *Artificial Intelligence*, Stuart Russell and Peter Norvig, Prentice Hall, 2003.

new jobs are being issued precisely from new applications and also because some jobs could not be so easily replaced by a machine.[32]

In spite of all of the wonderful expectations offered by AI there is a worrying trend to generate a rampant collective control on our individual liberties. We have previously mentioned what currently happens in China but the trend is universal. For instance a permanent control through satellites of the full car traffic in order to detect those which do not respect the speed limitations has been introduced (in France and elsewhere). This is a pretty good excuse to tap into personal and private lives. With such data it becomes easily feasible for Big Brother to spy and record the whereabouts of anybody — to what use?

5.6. AI in the art of medicine

At the beginning the art of medicine of Hippocrates or even Gallien was rather crude: clyster, bleeds were used without any previous diagnostics and followed by empirical remedies. Moreover these cures were reserved for rich people able to buy the plants of herbalism.

With the modern times came democratization, standardization, a diversification of the medications following standards of active principles and doses. That still remains quite empirical, approximate, and subjective. The question of compatibility between the drugs remains an issue.

The future is an open door to GAFAM. The current trend is to improve the database in order to get detailed information about any patient and his medical history. The physician will have to become accustomed to discussion with the machine. The pharmaceutical industry will have to implement a production of "tailor-made medicines" to take care of the individual complexity of the body. AI will provide the rationality of statistics to each particular case. This is a future not already reached but may soon be accessible.

As postulated by Larry Page, at Google, "any problem, as complex as it could, may find a solution provided that the database is large enough and the computer powerful enough". Eric Topol[33] for his own part foresees that "deep medicine" will soon triumph over diabetes with future

---

[32] *The Lights in the Tunnel: Automation, Accelerating Technology and the Economy of the Future*, Martin Ford, CreateSpace Independent Publishing Platform, 2009.

[33] *The Creative Destruction of Medicine*, Eric Topol, Basic Books, New York, 2012.

predictive medicine whereas AI assisted robotization will improve precision in surgical operations. This last point has been strongly supported by a NIH budget of $207 million to help the "Precision Medicine Initiative".

All of those changes will assuredly erode the relationship with the doctor who will have to adapt to the new context of the "wireless health": smart watch app with a deep learning algorithm to detect atrial fibrillation, diabetic retinopathy automatically diagnosed by a machine, specific algorithms for the radiologists or ophthalmologists. Obviously this might not compare to the human intelligence but the power is there to integrate a multitude of data and give a complete result through an unfailing memory. The pinnacle of AI is being fully autonomous and compatible with the patient. Of course this also shows little respect for personal intimacy but that was already the case with a human physician even if more confidential.

5.7. *AI and medicine in society*

There is already a vicious cycle between the needs and the means in medicine: the population of elderly (even centenarians[34]) is increasing steadily which requires more and more ubiquitous cares and services to the point that some are afraid a possible Malthusianism would soon prevail. On the other hand the studies of medicine in universities are lasting longer and longer to take into account the progressing volume of knowledge in the field. All of that leads to a shortage of physicians. The patient also begins to require more and more sophisticated an approach and the recourse to AI will become mandatory by which time a dedicated teaching for doctors will be required.

A possible answer could be to shorten the studies or, even better, to deliberately teach them in a supervised AI contribution in order to help to diagnose, adapt the cures and remember the therapy.

5.8. *AI in biology*

Biology is a very active field of research and the applications are quite impressive. That is the reason why we can find so many transhumanists involved in that domain.

---

[34]Fillard, *Longevity.*

Genetics has come to reveal the secrets (some of them) of the DNA molecule and now let the possibility with CRISPR cas9 to cut and replace faulty elements. This opens the door for a possible anti-ageing therapy or even "rejuvenation" or "ageing reversal". Stem cells also offer limitless possibilities to act on the brain constitution and contribute to a course on intelligence. Competition has arisen with Elon Musk who advocates for a hybridization with integrated circuits directly implanted in the brain. Also to be mentioned is the crazy idea of an Italian surgeon to bluntly graft a head on another body!

Heart and blood are in the same game to find a biological equivalent. Would all of that culminate in an artificial creation of a Man as a standard or personalized "improved" model?

In the long term there are some goals for hypothetical AI take-off scenarios. Social intelligence will benefit from the "affective computing" (Rosalind Picard),[35] ability to simulate empathy and give appropriate response for those emotions.

About the "theory of mind", there are no objective criteria for knowing whether an intelligent agent is sentient (that it has conscious experience); subjective determination is a "hard problem". Computationalism is the idea that "human mind or human brain (or both) is an information processing system and that thinking is a form of computing."[36]

---

[35] *Affective Computing*, Rosalind Picard, MIT Press, 1995.
[36] *Mind Children*, Hans Moravec, Harvard University Press, 1988.

Chapter Seven

Energy and Civilizations

The basis of the transhumanist "philosophy" relies on the hypothesis of an uninterrupted acceleration of the technical means induced by scientific progress. This evolution supposes a genuine need for energy; although this point is seldom evoked in the discussions by transhumanists, it remains a fundamental requirement to support any important change. We are not dealing here with purely philosophically-minded people but with trivial realities of the material world.

In that respect it must be remembered that robots of any kind are voracious in their consumption of energy, let alone the calorigenic data centers. Energy is a prerequisite of our future whatever it should be. This thirst of ever more available energy is, by no means, a new feature (and fundamental limitation) but persists from the beginning of humanity; this is to the point that each new civilization inevitably has been triggered by a necessary discovery of a new source of energy (and *vice versa*). This time we are desperately looking for a new source of energy to give to 2.0 its very dimension in the post-humanist world, especially if a Singularity is to occur someday. Augmented intelligence (artificial or not) is of no use if it does not fit with the corresponding power to act.

The brain is the human organ which burns the most energy in the body; is that essentially to stimulate intelligence? Would an increased "super intelligence" require substantially boosting blood flow and augmenting the oxygenation yield[1] to face the needs?

---

[1] Would this deserve a comment from Kurzweil?

1. What is Energy?

That is the first question worth asking because this is neither a physical object nor a philosophical one. Actually, Power or Energy are virtual concepts (as well as Information) intended to materialize something immaterial, evanescent, which supports physical-chemical transformations in our environment. Something like an expressed balance of a reaction. Some various manifestations of Energy are suggested in Figure 7.1.

Energy has no materiality *per se*. Nobody ever saw a KWh or a Calorie jumping from a radiator even if the indirect effect is perceptible and even if such an Energy is measurable! The units are largely diversified depending on the context at issue and any equivalence and transposition can be easily obtained.

Physicists are familiar with the various mathematical formulation of Energy, from the initial kinetic energy of Leibniz ($E = 1/2mv^2$), to the famous Einstein's formula ($E = mc^2$) through the equivalence principle of Carnot ($E = JQ$).

In order to implement Energy, whatever the aim, we need to benefit from a "potential" source of energy, ready to be used or later available. It is possible to juggle with energy transformations but not create energy from scratch. Energy does spontaneously exist in Nature, on a large scale, but not often directly usable (wind, tides, geothermal energy). Energy is

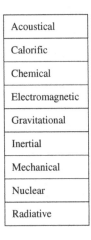

| Acoustical |
| Calorific |
| Chemical |
| Electromagnetic |
| Gravitational |
| Inertial |
| Mechanical |
| Nuclear |
| Radiative |

Figure 7.1.   Various aspects of energy.

part of the Universe, energy is life. What could be the impact of the discovery of an unexpected new energy source on the outbreak of a Singularity? Would that not be a prerequisite?

Up to now our understanding of the surrounding world has improved noticeably, thanks to the physicists. However, comparing to what remains to be understood, some would think we still remain in the Stone Age due to the many mysteries we have yet to decipher. Among these mysteries is the very way to master and store energy and eventually find new forms more adapted to our needs.

For instance, let us consider the fantastic gravitational energy expended by the Moon to stir up the tides all over the planet. Would it not be possible to benefit more directly of it?

Space is sometimes mentioned by transhumanists as a way to promote "improved" humans in a drastically different environment (Mars or even Pluto are on the list of possible planets worth "colonizing"). In such a context Energy would be the first critical requirement.

2. Energy as a Trigger for Civilizations

Once upon a time, a Cro-Magnon had the idea to bring back in his cave a torch lighted somewhere by a thunderbolt. After the Cro-Magnon's family had overcome the initial fright, they understood the benefits of such an amazing serendipity: light and heat were available at home on pain of tending the fire with dry wood for days and nights. They learned how to cook meat and a civilization of fire began where fire was essential to the point that men were ready to go to war over a lack of fire. So they discovered Energy and the corresponding constraints to face to keep it available: permanently going to collect dry deadwood.

Following the millennia new kinds of Energy were sought, classified, transformed, and finally used. Each time, these discoveries have had a direct impact on our life conditions, our comfort, our health, our civilizations and still more our living expectations. From the beginning Energy has behaved as a vector of the evolution of our civilizations.

In Chapter 1 (Table 1.1), reproduced here as Figure 7.2, we have tried to gather schematically some essential steps in the management of energy in history, since the beginning. The mastering of fire has been the very

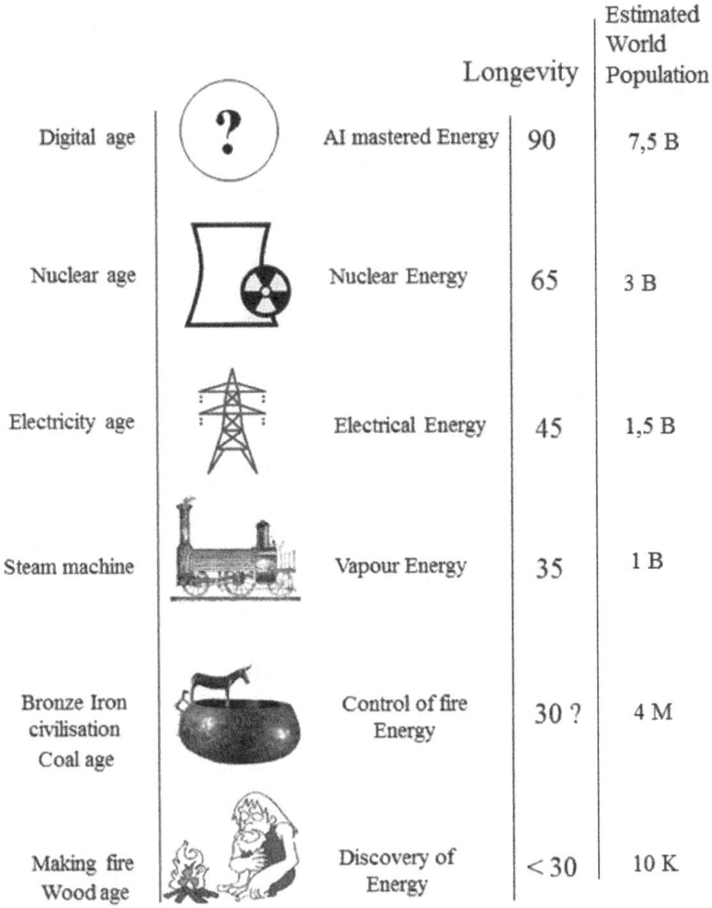

		Longevity	Estimated World Population
Digital age	?	AI mastered Energy	90	7,5 B
Nuclear age		Nuclear Energy	65	3 B
Electricity age		Electrical Energy	45	1,5 B
Steam machine		Vapour Energy	35	1 B
Bronze Iron civilisation Coal age		Control of fire Energy	30 ?	4 M
Making fire Wood age		Discovery of Energy	< 30	10 K

Figure 7.2. Some main steps in the evolution, resulting from a new source of energy.

starting point. Each step of these discoveries have induced a corresponding important improvement in our life conditions thus resulting in a progression in our longevity and correspondingly the extent of the global population. This table ends with a ? concerning the present "Digital Age" still waiting for its own serendipity.

To some extent these steps might be considered individual Singularities as long as they have induced irreversible changes in the course of our ways of life, in our knowledge, even in our inner selves. Each time a new serendipity cumulates with the previous one in order to construct the "progress" of our evolution. This was not enough to drastically change Man as transhumanists would hope now, but they assuredly contributed to bring us where we are today.

Other steps in Energy have not been mentioned here, although they were crucial, such as, for instance, the domestication of animals (oxen or horses) or the mastering of the wind for sail boats. They all generated irreversible changes in our destinies, waiting for the "Great Leap" announced by the transhumanists. This culmination could be tentatively sketched in the graph shown in Figure 7.3.

This situation is analogous to what Kurzweil named a succession of Paradigms, behaving in an accumulation of single S-curves. Ronald Hanson meanwhile emphasizes "a small number of exponential growth modes which correspond to the hunting, farming, and industrial areas. This is driven by the appearance of new technologies that change the structure and scale of the economy." With "[a] logistic-like limitation of increase of growth rate within each mode."

It is also worth noting that Energy is not given for nothing; Energy is an expensive good to be used sparingly and keeping heed of the consequences (risks, pollution, and so on).

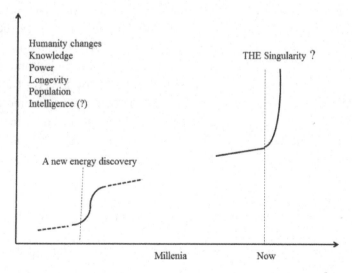

Figure 7.3. Cumulated singularities until the last one to come.

3. Singularity *vs* Singularities

Singularity, in some way, means a threshold, a discontinuity, in the collective behavior of humanity. In the past all the observed "singularities" effectively come from a discovery of a new kind of energy which makes possible new technical opportunities; afterwards, these opportunities generated a wave of welfare for individuals, as a consequence.

There is already an example of a singularity in our physical world: the quantum limit of the speed of light (or more conveniently the "celerity"). Matter or even electro-magnetic or gravitational waves are limited to speeds lower than the light celerity "c" whatever the energy involved to accelerate them. This is a universal limit we can asymptotically approach but never cross. Even neutrinos, the mass of which is close to zero, cannot cross this limit.

Physicists, for a long time, desperately tried to emphasize what could be something faster than "c" until Einstein[2] developed his "theory of relativity". This is a real singularity which, from the outset, consistently belongs to our physical world. Nobody knows if "there is a life behind"! Of course this example is certainly no more than a twist to illustrate the word "Singularity".

In the special case of a potential unique Singularity to come (as emphasized by Kurzweil), things would not be the same. The threshold would arise from a burst in Science, in the domains of Biology (health, ageing, or genetics) and Computers (databases and AI deep learning). The individuals would, then, be individually transformed from bottom up and their intelligence would be enhanced (or replaced) by the AI of a computer. The incidence of the change in global society would come afterwards if the process was to be spread all over. Then, the mechanism would be quite different. Of course Energy would be concerned in various ways but rather as a consequence of the change, not a direct motivation as it was the case before.

To implement energy, it is mandatory to dispose of a preliminary "potential" source that would be available and ready to be used, but

---

[2] Without going into details, the key issue is that "c" does not depend on the inertial referential involved.

Energy is fugitive and it is not easy to keep it in a box! Energy cannot be obtained freely from nothing. Energy is a valuable good.

All along the millennia, one sought, all the time, to outperform the simple wood fire. Human ingenuity is a result of this quest for progress. The Bronze Age emerged from the use of coal instead of wood, quickly followed by metallurgy and corresponding countless artifacts and useful instruments. Modernity must be built by accumulation of knowledge, step by step.

Today, coal is considered as too polluting and its use restrained by the benefit of other possible sources to produce our vital electricity. Energy currently has to be clean, abundant, and cheap (some say ecological)!

Along this narrative, the common term is "fire", which remains a critical necessity. We are forever fighting to appropriate "fire" (i.e. oil) from our neighbors and the "Quest for Fire" is still there.

4. The Current Balance Sheet of Resources

Then came the era of the machines and the corresponding upheaval; steam appeared as an intermediate substrate of energy for any kind of machines, even for nuclear reactors! Then the human possibilities were multiplied through the contribution of electricity. This kind of energy gave birth, for the first time, to a new possibility of long distance communications since the historical message launched by Samuel FB Morse on his telegraph, in 1938: "Attention the Universe! By kingdoms! Right wheel!". No need for transhumanist philosophers to comment about the future from that innovation!

But machines, as powerful as they can be, behave in a very voracious way when it comes to consuming energy. Pipelines and tankers cross continents and the oceans to convey oil or gas home, all over the planet. Some say this is "the blood of the civilizations". If that runs out or if the electrons go on strike that would be the end of our civilizations!

Water steam has long been a very useful and versatile kind of energy that has animated a wealth of energy transformations to switch from heat to mechanical movement through pistons or turbines. So the boat engines made it possible, for the first time, to get rid of the vagaries of the wind whereas locomotives allowed long haul transport of heavy loads.

This steam was also very useful to generate a new kind of energy: the electricity generated in power stations all over the world. This kind of energy is very practical due to its ability to be transferred and distributed according to needs. Even nuclear power plants proceed with such a cascade of transformations. To some extent electricity can also be stored in batteries, which is very significant in many local and limited situations.

Despite all of these improvements arising from "fire", one needs now even more energy and an unlimited source was discovered in the very depth of matter: the nuclear energy which is called upon to abundantly contribute in our constantly rising quest for Terawatts of power. This was the last tread on the ladder for reaching new civilizations, at the moment when questions began to be asked about a future exhaustion of the usual natural resources.

The choice for the U_{235} material (or Pu_{239} artificially grown) in the reactors was deduced from previous military technology derived from the nuclear bomb. In spite of the famous Chernobyl accident, there are now hundreds of reactors in the world which are trying to satisfy our thirst for energy. We have now entered the era of the atom which brings us a unique contribution even if many people are afraid. But it must be understood that any extensive source of energy, whatever it comes from, will inescapably pose a hazard of the same dimension. That is quite inescapable.

5. What About a Possible Future?

Our future, whatever the ideas of the transhumanist philosophers and whatever the dreams of the ecologists, will require much more energy. Great hopes have been placed on the "fusion" phenomenon of light elements and an international megaproject is on the way: ITER[3] is under experimentation in France (Cadarache).

A fusion reaction proceeds from the collision between light nuclei as Hydrogen isotopes, contrary to fission which comes from the fracture of

---

[3] The "International Thermonuclear Experimental Reactor" is, as of now, an experimental prototype only intended to test the many technical solutions before dealing with a real operational plant.

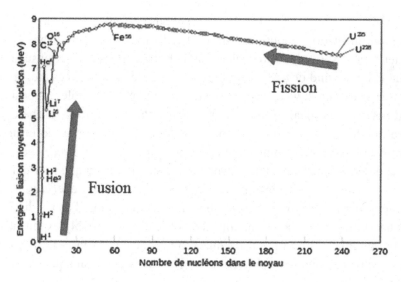

Figure 7.4.   Comparative energetic balances of Fission and Fusion.

a heavy one. As indicated in Figure 7.4, the yield of the Fusion reaction well exceeds that of the Fission but the way to implement it is more complex. The control of the reaction is quite touchy and that is the reason why fusion has only been successfully used in the thermonuclear bombs where there is no need of a control or containment; the available energy is blown over and that's it. This constitutes a very technical subject which is hardly approached by the transhumanist philosophers, even if a success in this issue could be a real breakthrough for our electricity supply.

Many attempts have been performed to catch this dragon's tail but unsuccessfully up to now. The experimental set ups generally proposed, consist of a toroidal vacuum chamber where hydrogen atoms are accelerated and injected to generate plasma and thus favor the reaction. But this situation behaves in a very unstable way and is rather uneasy to be managed or extract energy. ITER currently represents the last chance to implement a future power station on the scale needed for the 2.0 civilization. It is foreseen that the radioactivity and corresponding wastes would be much limited compared to the fission solution. This would be a convenient argument to convince the general opinion that this source of energy is not so dangerous, all things considered.

Many people are afraid of this tremendous dependence on the nuclear solution and worry about the safety of the future humanity. They have better turn to soft, renewable, clean, and cheap sources of energy such as solar cells or wind or tide power plants. However these sources are, up to now, rather limited: weak capacity, intermittent, unpredictable, expensive, and not so ecological to implement. Clearly these solutions can be of a great interest in many specific, local situations but in no way to bring a universal large scale complement to our present global 2.0 need. Thus we remain dependent on nuclear power for a while, transhumanists or not.

Enthusiasts for nuclear power in the 1950s promised energy "too cheap to meter". We need to keep this long history in mind as we discuss the latest phase — a belief that the geometrically, or possibly exponential increase in the ability of our machines to make calculations will result in an equally profound magnification of our knowledge and power. This dream has lately been revived with the promise of genetic engineering to follow a similar development. David Brin said that "the notion that a new level of existence or a more appealing state of being, might be achieved by means of knowledge and skill." The dream still remains valid.

Now 2.0 has come but not any new form of energy which could be on the required scale to feed the data centers amongst many other energy-hungry consumers. If Anthropocene has to progressively vanish (as suggested by many transhumanists) and if a new age of "Robotcene" is dawning, the unsatisfied quest for more energy may restrain this transition.

6. Energy, Technical Singularities, and the World Beyond

Some think that Technical Singularities would result from a burst in intelligence which helps implement new serendipities among which energy plays a prominent role. Some transhumanist philosophers even discussed these opportunities and their applications. Vernor Vinge was the first to coin the term "Technical Singularity" in 1993 to strictly specify the technical origin of the change expected.

Singularity is the key point in the discussions about a possible post-Singularity world. Surely human population, energy, space, and computing power are, at this stage, useful for future progress. However, their influence on development is difficult to describe with a simple formula;

the Singularity idea exerts a powerful intellectual and imaginative attraction … and deserves a critical examination (after Max More).

Some (as David Brin) argue that any change would require first a brain transfer in a machine to get the level required but even in such a situation the change will not be immediate: "If uploads cannot be created, then the Singularity will be delayed until the software problem has been solved or uploading becomes possible. The Earth would not be transformed into a giant computer in a few days."

As a matter of fact, the technical progresses which drive toward a Singularity mainly rely on the improvements in the technology of the transistors which have become smaller and smaller following the yet uninterrupted Moore's law! So the throng of these bugs became denser and denser in the integrated circuits but hopefully also less and less individually demanding in energy. Nevertheless the global energy consumption of the full systems still steadily increased substantially.

Would an electronic Singularity be expected to outreach the wall of the quantum limitations? Great hopes are currently founded on what is called "Q-bits": a kind of atomic structure managed by pure Quantum Physics. Several different configurations are already competing,[4] ranging from superconductive circuits to laser driven ion-traps or photonics light particles. Each solution comes with its advantages and also its drawbacks; this to the point that the final challenger still remains unknown.

The previous use of a binary logic would, then, be abandoned in favor of a more subtle management of the quantum incertitude. Q-bits would no longer be limited in a 0/1 decision choice, as usual, but open to any combination of gradation between. It could thus become possible to favor parallel algorithms and get a huge step ahead in the speed of calculation.

This miraculous prospect does not appear without serious drawbacks. The first one is theoretical and relies on the new logic to be implemented from scratch. Nothing is certain at this moment and even the basic quantum requirements are yet to be assessed. The second one stands more at the practical level: such superconducting Q-bits, in order to properly be

---

[4] For more detailed information see "Business bets on a Quantum Leap", Robert Hackett, *Fortune*, May 21, 2019.

operated, will require to be put at a stable temperature very close to the absolute zero. This is neither easy nor cheap!

Many expensive research programs are busily underway with big companies all over the world: IBM, Microsoft, Intel, Google, NASA … and, not to be forgotten, Huawei, among others! Some prototypes are already available (D-Wave Company) but not definitively adopted industrially.

Obviously, such a Quantum Leap would bring us beyond a Computer Singularity and that would play in the arms of the transhumanists with its immediate corresponding consequences in the various domains of finances, energy, AI as well as medicine … not to mention the ability to pierce the encryption of the Internet's data. Currently this is grounded more in hope than in results but quite a revolution is in perspective!

Let us remember 1947 when the transistor effect was discovered; nobody, at that time, would have bet a single cent on the future of this small three legged gimmick as a possible challenger of the well-established technology of the vacuum tubes … and yet, it took only two decades for lamps to be eliminated. So let us wait a decade more for further information about Q-bits!

If such a gadget is to be conveniently operated, then AI would find a frightening dimension, well beyond the limits of our human associated brains, and transhumanists would applaud the show!

7. Singularity or Apocalypse?

To anticipate the future it remains instructive to take a look at the past. Some transhumanists forecast that the change should be limited to a deep transformation (a Singularity, an event, a spike or even a "human Concept Horizon") of our human self; others imagine a deeper apocalyptic disruption concerning the whole planet or even the universe.

In the first situation transformation would apply to some (selected?) individuals, one after the other, whereas the second hypothesis would involve a collectivity or even the whole of humanity in a single catastrophe.

We do have to consider the various opinions formulated by also various transhumanists, few of them being concerned with the required energy to generate the change. In any case, we enter, here, the realm of pure hypothesis; each has his own vision of the issue. Many agree to assign a central role for the emerging AI but, once again, it is one thing to know, and another to be able to do (by this I mean, have enough energy to). Would a major Singularity be conceivable with the present availability of energy? That is not so sure. However, the emergence of a super intelligence has the great potential of being fundamentally game-changing for humanity (for good or ill).

Nevertheless, a lone super intelligence, or even a few, would not accelerate overall economic and technological development all that much.

For Damien Broderick, "within thirty years we will have the technology means to create superhuman intelligence. Shortly after, the human era will be ended.[5] Singularity is called 'the spike'. We have heard this sort of thing prophesized in literally apocalyptic religious revelations of the End Time and Rupture. It's a pity the timing coincides fairly closely with dates proposed by the superstitions."

Many authors have fitted human population to a similar hyperbolic growth curve where population would reach infinity at some time t. Technology grows proportional to population; what about energy?

Ronald Hanson said that the possibility of a Singularity, in contrast, creates "an opaque wall across the future" beyond which "things are completely unknowable".[6] Why? Because humans are to posthumans as "goldfishes" are to us.

Nick Boström, for his part, is a bit more skeptical: "I do not regard the Singularity as being a certainty, just one of the most likely scenarios (technological development, super intelligence, unpredictability). Some people have made unpredictability a defining feature of the Singularity."

Alexander Chislenko[7] (a theoretical biologist and philosopher) raised the point of a "dramatic turning point" he found in the book of his father Leonid.[8] He was fascinated by the "global scaling theory" revealing a

---

[5] *A Fire Upon the Deep*, Vernor Vinge, Tom Doherty Associates, 1992.
[6] Vinge, see above note 5.
[7] "A critical discussion of Vinge's Singularity concept", David Brin, Damien Broderick, Nick Boström, Alexander "Sasha" Chislenko, Robin Hanson, Max More, Michael Nielsen, and Anders Sandberg, in *The Transhumanist Reader*, 2013, p. 402.
[8] *The Structure of Fauna and Flora in Connection with the Sizes of the Organisms*, Leonid Leonidovich Chislenko, Moskow Universty Press, 1981 (in Russian).

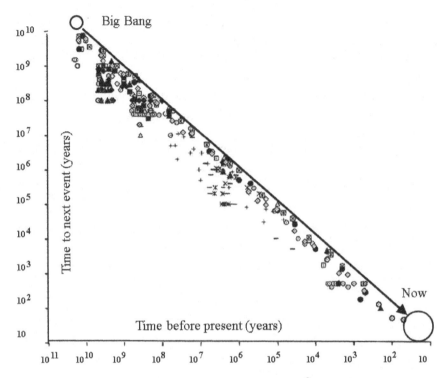

Figure 7.5. The famous diagram proposed by R Kurzweil[9] to show the evolution of the delays between each new event from the geological beginning to present.

logarithmic scale-invariance behavior. So he proposed a drawing showing that "on the logarithmic scale the complexity doubling periods reside on a single straight line that laconically touch the X-axis at the 2030 year mark."[10] Then we would be close to the deadline!

The magic of the log/log scale diagram spread out and reached Ray Kurzweil[11] who used it to gather the delays between the most important events and canonical milestones from the geological ages up to present. The following is his explanation of his diagram seen in Figure 7.5: "the following plot combines fifteen different lists of key events. Since

---

[9] I, unfortunately, do not have the means to check the validity of Kurzweil's data, so we have to blindly trust him!

[10] No wise mathematician would be able to explain how a straight line on a log/log plot could reach an X-axis which only has an indicative meaningless position.

[11] Kurzweil, *Singularity,*

different thinkers assign different dates to the same event, and different lists include similar or overlapping events selected according to different criteria, we see an expected 'thickening' of the trend line due to the noisiness (statistical variance) of this data; the overall trend, however, is very clear."

Kurzweil also adds: "In technology, if we go back fifty thousand years, not much happened over one-thousand-years period. But in the recent past, we see new paradigms, such as the World Wide Web, progress from inception to mass adoption ... within only a decade."

Indeed, this plot is astonishingly striking (and a bit frightening too) as long as the consistency and the correctness of the data are accepted. This linear alignment clearly demonstrates a hyperbolic dependence[12] of the events, starting at the very beginning, close to the Big Bang,[13] with a very wide-spaced evolution but powerful changes along millions of millennia, to reach an accelerating sequence of steps of weaker amplitude (and weaker energies involved) which pile up rapidly with shorter delays between them.

To conclude Kurzweil said: "This acceleration matches our commonsense observations. A billion years ago, not much happened over the course of even one million years. But a quarter-million years ago epochal events such as the evolution of our species occurred in time frames of just one hundred thousand years."

More symbolically Vernor Vinge invented the "Technical Singularity" induced by the superhuman intelligence:[14] "within thirty years, we will have the technological means to create superhuman intelligence. Shortly after, the human era will be ended." This is in agreement with the pessimistic view of Fukuyama who said that Singularity is "the most dangerous idea in the world."

All of this conveniently shows that, through the opinion of all these philosophers (and scientists too), something big is to be expected in a rather near future.

---

[12] This behavior is in no way exponential as mistakenly said by Kurzweil but clearly hyperbolical, which is even worse!

[13] Would this Big Bang be considered as the Initial Singularity emerging from something before?

[14] Vinge proposed, as a definition that Technical Singularity would result from "increasing efficiency in the use, processing, transport of matter, energy and information".

Part III
Problems to be Solved

Chapter Eight

Man and Men, Issues To Be Faced

Humanity is in no case a collection of identical human beings. They differ from one continent to another, within a continent and, at an even smaller scale, inside a given society. Each enjoys his own personality which is quite unique. What is established to be appropriate for one will not necessarily suit the other. This point is rarely addressed by transhumanists; how to get it?

1. Transhumanism is Concerned with Man but the Issue is Men

Science will be soon be able to change the inner nature of human beings, that much is certain, but there are so many ways to choose what we are looking for! There is not a single answer to the question. Transhumanists often raise issues but seldom propose solutions.

Following established forecasts, the world population is intended to continue its stable growth and could reach a slight inflexion around the middle of the 21st century as indicated in Figure 8.1. If transhumans are to appear soon it is hard to imagine that the transformation could affect a large majority of them in a jiffy; then there will likely be a more or less extended period where Trans and non-Trans would have to coexist. There will be a class of "privileged Supermen"[1] amongst ordinary humans.

---

[1] Or, maybe, "privileged robots"?

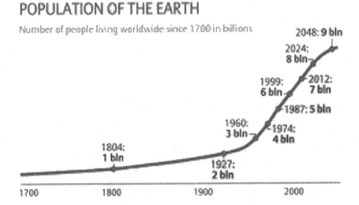

Figure 8.1. Forecasted evolution of the world population.

That raises a lot of questions that mix together. What exactly could it mean to be a transhuman: improved intellectual means? Rejuvenated? Enhanced physical performances? Computer compatible? Would that change result from a hierarchical selection? Would the change follow a kind of "menu" to get adapted to a specific activity? Would it be gender indifferent? One can hardly imagine that the "improvement" would cover every domain of human knowledge at the same time! Would there be first some "prototypes", some "β Version" in order to reach, later, an improved version?

A possibility could be (and this is a likely one) that the transhuman transformation would not result from a specific individual change implemented as a new technological operation in the body (biological or electronic implants) but rather result from the global accepted evolution of our way of life, one step after the other in order for them to become assimilated in daily use. Not of a sudden revolution or Singularity: a prefiguration of that being e.g. the current usage of the smartphone, so easily accepted by children; no need for a particular initiation, it becomes an extension of their self and allows sharing serendipities at school.

At some point, these children might become comparably more skilled with the phone than older people; this could be a matter of getting (for some lucky ones at least) a "super-assisted-intelligence", with instant access to Internet. Knowledge no longer has to be memorized; Internet is there to provide it instantly. No need to have a chip implanted in the brain, the phone does the job as an artificial duplicate of the personality. The smartphone innovation has reached the collectivity as a whole. Would children already be transhumans?

But the story does not end there! Adults too are already victims of the phone mania, it is enough to look at the streets, the supermarket or any waiting room and count the number of people busy with their device, not paying any attention to the world around! They are in their own virtual world and that is just the very beginning for the "connected" people.

Time will come when Google will know everything about everyone. Then, through this vital phone, Google will provide you with every useful (or not) information in real time to help you (in a first step) in any situation of your life. In a second step of the invasion, Google will decide for you the best advisable choice (economic, emotional, political, or else) you have to follow and you will assuredly become a confident e-puppet of Google.

Meanwhile, Transhumanist philosophers have developed a principle of "Extropy" (not opposed to the notion of Thermodynamical Entropy) defined as "the extent of a living or organizational system's intelligence, functional order, vitality, and capacity and drive for improvement". That's obvious Dr Watson! Would that help clarify the issue?

Concerning the observed increasing life span, it does not take a firm believer of transhumanism to see that the continuous evolution of our performance is due to the multiple improvements induced, over and over, in our daily life, all people concerned, (in health care, monitoring, preventive medicine, food quality and control, information…) rather than a particular sudden miraculous discovery about our DNA or AI which could generate a "Superman" as a "life after life".[2] That progress does occur everyday and regardless of the verbiage of the philosophers. It is purely technical.

Some argue that "even if aging is conquered, our biological bodies are too fragile to ensure our survival against accident and mayhem over very

---

[2] "Life expansion media", Natasha Vita-More in *The Transhumanist Reader*.

long periods of time".[3] The only solution to reach long term survival remains the "uploading"of our minds and personality onto a different substrate. In any case we know better how to support a machine than a human body!

2. Personal Identity vs Enhancement

However in order to "upload" a mind, it is necessary to first define what a mind is made of. Scores of philosophers, scholars or distinguished thinkers have been trying for a long time (may be millennia) to provide a definition of what is intended by the self, the personality, the personal identity. In vain! The mind is so fugitive, so plastic, so changing, that coming up with a holistic description remains illusory and *a fortiori* to translate it in a machine.

2.1. *Uploading a mind*

Nevertheless transhumanists have not given up hope to succeed, at least partly if not wholly. There is no absolute reality of what a particular mind (at a particular instant t) could be summarized in a snapshot. We do also know that every mind is sensitive to any external sensation or chemical influence. Some drugs are even well known for their curative (or at least sedative) effects on "deviant" spirits.

Now there is a dream to go further, to modify, to enhance, or to reinvent a self from scratch. This remains presumptuous but that is on track. Transhumanists embrace projects of radical cognitive enhancement that would change every constitutive element of consciousness to a malleable fiction in order to create an ideal self.

Giulio Prisco[4] is persuaded that the dream of achieving an indefinite lifespan will come sooner or later to reality through a "transcendent engineering". It lies in leaving biology behind and getting to a new cybernetic phase of our evolution. The ultimate technology for immortality will make

---

[3] "Human enhancement, the cognitive sphere", Max More in *The Transhumanist Reader*.
[4] "Engineering transcendence", Giulio Prisco, December 1, 2006. Available at: http://giulioprisco.blogspot.com/2006/12/engineeringtranscendence.html

possible mind uploading in a machine by means of new high-performance substrates. Such a post-biological embodiment process would present options which could be chosen as pure software to live without a physical body. This would exactly fit, for instance, with the rugged space requirements. To go yet further, some other transhumanists even evoke a possibility that science and technology would be able to, in some way, resurrect the dead and ask the frequent question: do we already live in a simulation? In such a case the other question follows: who is running the simulation of men's societies?

2.2. *The self to be enhanced*

Enlightenment[5] values were built around the presumption that humans are autonomous individuals not defined as being given a God's immaterial and supernatural soul. It is our capacity to think which makes us able to be a "person". David Hume,[6] for his part, argues that "the self is also an illusion created by the contiguity of sense perceptions and thoughts. The self is merely a bundle or collection of different perceptions which succeed one another". But more recently Thomas Metzinger[7] proposes that "neuroscience shows that the "self-y" feeling is simply a useful heuristic that our minds create, without any underlying reality".

The transhumanist project is concerned with reaching cognitive and biological enhancements. That could lead to an extended life where personal identity could be adapted but also where radical changes to memory, cognition, etc. would radically challenge our notion of self. However Nick Boström admits that "certain information patterns are conserved, such as memories, values, attitudes, and emotional dispositions and so long as there is causal continuity so that earlier stages of yourself help determine later stages of yourself."

Such a psychological continuity theory advocated by Kurzweil has been dubbed "Paternalism" in order to preserve "the memory of a flow of

---

[5] "Essay concerning human understanding", John Locke, 1689.

[6] *A Treatise of Human Nature*, David Hume, 1739. Available at: http://www.gutenberg.org/ ebooks/4705

[7] *The Ego Tunnel: The Science of the Mind and the Myth of the Self*, Thomas Metzinger, New York Basic Books, 2009.

mental states leading to the present is maintained". So if the mind is transferred in a computer it would have to remember the process leading to the change. Then, these "transformationalists" agree in some way to change the mind provided that the change does not affect the continuity of the self and that "the path from humanness to 'godlike' post-humanity should be gradual"! That's an ambiguous catch-22!

There is also the issue of the duplication of the enhancement in order to account for the infinite diversity of the selves and the diversity of the possible multiple copies coming from a same individual at different stages of its evolution.

Of course, this is a kind of "mythology" as stated by Prisco and dubbed "The Turing Church" to emphasize the key role of the substrate independent mentality. This resembles a quasi-religious formulation of the transhumanism developed by Robert Geraci.[8]

All the references I have gathered with their various speculations are intended to give an appraisal of the diversity of the transhumanist visions. And, to conclude the discussion following Max More: "if there is no real self and no real humanity then we are left with the question of whether we want to collectively pretend that we do exist, and if so, to what end?".

3. Increasing World Population

In the past centuries, life expectancy steadily rose but the acceleration came in the middle of the 20th one. We are now seeing more people living up to 90 years and above with centenarians[9] beginning to flock in the obituary columns of the newspapers. This is a new phenomenon introduced by the transhumanist as the beginning of a new era for a humanity which is soon intended to live 150, 200 years or even more; that is a pretty nice view, especially if the physical and intellectual fitness are secured. But that does not come without bringing up serious issues and drawbacks to be overcome. Up to now centenarians were considered as individual exceptional abnormalities but this will change as it becomes a real issue for the collectivity of men (or women!).

---

[8] *Apocalyptic AI: Visions of Heaven in Robotics, Artificial Intelligence and Virtual Reality*, Robert Geraci, New York University Press, 2010.
[9] Fillard, *Longevity*.

From the past, people became familiar with legendary biblical super-centenarians such as Methuselah but there was no civil register to record the performance and so serious doubts prevail. There was no way to check it. Today the record still belongs to Jeanne Calment (122 years) but voices are now heard to contest this!

The great hope for accessing a possible reversal of the ageing phenomenon relies on the control of the billions of individual cells housed in our body. Ageing is viewed to come from the decline of some of these cells which become "senescent" and stop working properly and even perturb the neighboring cells. That would come from the natural wear and tear of the DNA molecule and its "telomere". The solution then could be to reprogram or replace the damaged cells using stem cells grown *in vitro*. Some encouraging results have been obtained on mice but a transposition to humans is still a long way to come.

As long as the brain is concerned, lots of experiments are reported which deal with rat brains (it is well known that rats are especially intelligent animals). The breakthrough of CRISPR cas9 discovery was used to partially restore the sight of rats blinded by a kind of disease which also affects humans. But the new genetic technique allows them to do this for the first time and could also lead to new treatments for a range of diseases associated with the ageing process.

Lu *et al.*[10] have studied the human frontal cortex of individuals ranging from 26 to 106 years of age. They were led to the identification of a set of genes whose expression was becoming altered after age 40. Then ageing must be considered as a lifelong process of cumulative changes that ultimately becomes evident at old age. Age related decline in the brain is supposed to begin soon at the end of adolescence.

The brain regions which provide newly produced neuron cells are in the hippocampus and the striatum. Then their activity must be stimulated to prevent brain deficiencies. A first discovery of a key factor of this activity has been found in rat's blood (GDF 11) and researchers say that the process could likely be transferable to humans.

---

[10] "Gene regulation and DNA damage in the ageing human brain", Tao Lu, Ying Pan, Shyan-Yuan Kao, Cheng Li, Isaac Kohane, Jennifer Chan, and Bruce A. Yankner, *Nature*, 429(6994), 883–891, 2004.

All of that leads to a better appraisal of the brain functioning and the possibility of getting means to prevent brain ageing and improve fitness in the elderly.

Currently the world population increases "naturally"; modern healthcare (and the quality of the food) becomes more widespread due to increasingly effective medical control which allows populations to get to a better physical condition and so "naturally" slowing the ageing process. This results in an increasing longevity and a consistent population growth. This tendency will be more and more sensitive as younger generations which have benefitted from these cares all along, will become older.

The more the populations get older (old timers!) the more they are susceptible to diseases which are specific to ageing such as cancer or Alzheimer's. Cancer, however, is in no way a new disease related to industrialization or pollution; the feeling of newness comes from the population coming of age and a better screening to identify the plague. In the year 1750 the life expectancy was still in the range of 30. The risk of dying from a cancer was much lower than dying from the many other causes active at that time; prostate cancer rarely appears before 60. "Natural death" no longer exists today; there is always an identified origin. Long ago Richard Feynman used to say: "It is one of the most remarkable things in all of the biological sciences there is no clue as to the necessity of death". He might have been a transhumanist forerunner!

3.1. *Present status and forecasts*

Clearly, societies are deeply inhomogeneous and even in a same society there are major differences between individuals in terms of cultural, social, economic, or instruction level. However, there is a noticeable tendency towards homogenization of behaviors and a still larger access to care so the inflection point of the global population growth is not imminent. The basic need to provide increasing amounts of food, cares, energy, facilities, education, and so on will become a major challenge in future. This is especially true for the elderly that need paraphernalia of care thus creating plenty of jobs for the younger.

In any case, some day, it will become necessary to stop the growth and even reduce the global population (like it or not) and find the ways and the means to do that without disturbing the social structure. This issue will become more complex with the foreseen emergence of a substantial population of centenarians! Today there are more than 17,000 centenarians (men and mainly women) in France, from only a hundred in 1900 (in France too); it is forecasted that (with given constant living condition) there will be 75,000 in 2030 and 270,000 to 560,000 in 2070!

This slowdown of the global population could come, one day, from the bottom up with the reduction of the birth rate (already sensitive in the developed countries), due to the demanding requirements of modern life that prompt young households not to have children.

That is a new society which is to be implemented with its advantages and drawbacks.

3.2. Retirees as an economical issue or a new market?

The growing life expectancy induces many materialistic issues which have rarely been taken into consideration by the transhumanist thinkers. Yet this is of utmost importance in the changes to be introduced to the way of life.

The first consequence of the extended life span is economic: retirement pensions have been, up to now, calculated to the sixties (or even before) on the basis of a 20 years mean life after retirement but presently the mean longevity already extends to the nineties which means 10 more years to pay by the pension funds; that's a lot.

The immediate response could be to charge senior pensions with an exceptional tax in order to discourage elders to live so long! Another way could be to let people work for longer, but most of them would likely not agree so easily, saying: "we have worked for years, that's enough; we want now to appreciate our last years, living the comfortable life that we have deserved". Or, a well-balanced negotiation to manage paid part time work? Perhaps even the eventuality of an accessible "rejuvenation" process could play a role to help the elderly keep in good shape and be active in the workforce.

In this view it can also be considered that these "potential retirees", even if well experimented after a long professional activity, will need a drastic recycling to keep into account the fantastically fast evolution of the science and technology (even the committed professors in the universities who have to teach the younger!). This recycling program will require recycling teachers and thus we have come full circle!

Another issue comes with the youth who would not agree to see their expected promotion to be so delayed by these irremovable seniors. The same applies with the youth who are looking for a first job, which has not been released by the Youngers. In this view there will be quite a "promotion jam" to be caused! Any policy changes should not be introduced all of a sudden but likely softly enough to keep the age pyramid satisfactorily balanced (even if extended upwards) taking into account the current slowdown of the birth rate.

Another problem arises if the pension funds are reduced (or not carefully planned): the seniors will have to fund their living from their previous savings or involve their children to contribute (assuming the cost of living becomes higher as Older ages. As a consequence children are deprived (or delayed) of their inheritance. This generates what is currently called the 4-2-1 issue, meaning that a single working individual has to support his (her) two parents as well as his (her) four grandparents when they all are alive (and down and out).

This scheme is already valid in China where the social evolution has been explosive for a recent while and a gray wave is set to crash.[11] It is expected that, by 2050, 330 million Chinese will be over age 65, but meanwhile the total population will peak at 1.44 billion in 2029 before an "unstoppable" decline. This situation has its origin in the one child policy introduced in 1980 by Mao in order to slow down a growing hungry population. Now things have drastically changed, China has entered a prosperous era and the government reversed that policy. Even if propaganda now exhort couples to "have children for the country", Chinese have now embraced a modern way of life which requires getting enough money for living. People enter universities for an extended period of

---

[11] "The gray wave set to clash", Charley Campbell, *Time*, February 18–25, 2019.

expensive studies then they get married later and are not fond of adding to their burden by having kids to raise. They have troubles with their new needs to make ends meet and this results in an economy crippled by unsustainable debts.

What is currently noted for China is also true to a certain extent in the U.S. or even in Europe when governments have started to think about the possibility of reducing pensions for the elderly which have become too costly.

3.3. *Increasing longevity and senescence*

Transhumanists forecast an increased longevity to be observed and seek to find solutions from the advances in the biological technologies or from the digital world.

An interesting biological prospect lies in the relentless progresses in growing artificial organs through cell cultures[12] and 3D printing. We still are in the very beginning of this technique but it's so promising to get, at one's disposal, a fully compatible kidney or liver or pancreas, ready to be grafted! Not to imagine the same thing with a heart or a brain (this is still science fiction, but how long more?); that should be the very Holy Grail and give the human a God's power!

In such a situation the human behavior would be quite similar to that of a car the parts of which are changed when they get worn and the car's lifetime is accordingly extended.

However, immortality, whatever the solution it comes from, is not forcibly to everyone's liking. As Daniel Callahan[13] puts it: "There is no known social good coming from the conquest of death." Francis Fukuyama added: "Yes absolutely." A society of people with "ageless bodies" might have significant downsides.

---

[12] *The Long Tomorrow: How Advances in Evolutionary Biology Can Help Us Postpone Aging*, Michael Rose, Oxford University Press, 2005.

[13] "Would doubling the human life span be a net positive or negative for us either as individuals or as a society?", Gregory Stock and Daniel Callahan, *Journal of Gerontology Series A*, 59(6), B554–B559, 2004.

3.4. *Recycling and rejuvenescence of the seniors*

As a matter of fact old geezers are most welcome in the workforce of a country, mainly for their acquired and valuable experience accumulated over the years; however Science and mainly Technology evolve at an accelerated speed especially with the digital means that need to be mastered. In that way Internet and the Massive Open Online Courses (MOOCs) might be of a real help. This requires a recyclable mind potentially capable of switching to a different field. So, specialized and adapted teaching techniques have to be widely developed. Transhumanist philosophers are rather silent about these social requirements which nevertheless are a consequence of the brain improvements they are so fond of.

Some advanced solutions they proposed are based on the enhancement of human abilities without any requirement of the person's biological body: teleoperation of personal robot could take place through what they call Avatars. These various kinds of "extended personality" would expand the opportunities for experiences outside the conventional system. That lies very close to the world of games and the relation with reality could be questionable even if large debates are already open.[14] If several Avatars could be operated by a single person at once they could be allowed a more or less large degree of autonomy and so might escape the conventional moral system, which can lead to worrisome situations.

Whatever the Avatar, this will require an adapted interface[15] with the concerned body. Some partial solutions are already proposed to animate a machine (artificial robot, arm or leg) moved through electrodes stuck on the body close to the path of a nerve or directly implanted in the frontal or parietal lobe. Hopefully human minds are not old fashioned CPUs fixed in limited operations but enjoy plasticity and adaptability to engineer own learning environments.

Then AI of the bot can take over to make the biological and the technological hands meet. This field of research is on a real expansion in order to bring help to disabled elderly and keep them active.

---

[14] "Transavatars", William Sims Bainbridge in *The Transhumanist Reader*.
[15] "Re-inventing ourself", Andy Clark in *The Transhumanist Reader*.

Presently the levels of technology are not sufficient to fully achieve the ambitious goals of a mind transfer; so converting the radical transhumanist ideas into practical applications are not readily accessible and still remains in the domain of research.

4. Current Social Issues

On the wake of the transhumanist speculative approach and goals, there remain few implications for action. However considerable peripheral progresses have been achieved that have enlightened our knowledge to the point that some scholars rang the bell of "hypothetical risks and apocalyptic imaginings". The "Proactionary Principle" has emerged to motivate a need for wise decisions about the achievement of new committed technologies and corresponding undesirable side effects at a social holistic level.

The Proactionary Principle is committed to promote scientific discoveries and technical innovations in order to improve the human condition and societies. This is well summarized by Max More: "Protect the freedom to innovate and progress while thinking and planning intelligently for collateral effects".

The wisdom of this principle is intended to guiding the decision-making by the smartest procedures and to counter-balance the paradox of the Precautionary Principle which focuses only on the dangers and restricts any action at the social level. Then objectivity is to prevail to include "risk analysis, economics and the psychology of the decision-making and verifying the forecasting methods" (also Max More). It can be noted that there is a noticeable tendency in our worried current societies to be excessively cautious, bureaucratic, or socially sclerotic.[16]

That also means that we must remain open to the implications to societies as a whole given the current changes. This is not so easy because societies are complex systems made up of individuals (also complex). A key role is currently played by the media (TV, Facebook, Internet, and so on), trying to keep the individuals in the same mold of thought. It is through the media that knowledge is shared and must be discussed.

---

[16] For instance some people could be skeptical about some 2.0 hazards such as Climate Warming, CO_2 dangers or nuclear power stations that could lead to our extinction.

Concerning more especially the transhumanists, there is a debate or even a divide between those who promote enhancements and others who suggest the potentiality of social concerns. Some worry that the choices offered for improvement would not be available to enough people and argue that in any case the range of possibilities will be less than the range offered by the natural selection. We are now reaching the point where we may be able to transform ourselves in something other. This penetration into our inner space might change us all.

The current discussion about enhancement in general does not so much involve the medical safety and protection of the germline but rather philosophy and even religion from the perspective of the vision of the human future. The fear is that we could gradually cease to be who we have always been and also enter in a conflict between the enhanced and the unenhanced; and also exacerbate "the existing inequalities between the rich and the poor" (Nigel Cameron, president of the Center for Policy on Emerging Technologies) with "as much romantic interest in each other as a current human would have for a chimpanzee!" (Lee Silver,[17] Princeton University biologist).

To date, the original term "transhumanist" developed initially by Julian Huxley supports the idea of the techno-cultural improvement of human beings, in particular the cognitive function. They advocate a coming techno-social Singularity and the corresponding cognitive enhancement which is even referred by James Hughes[18] as a "spiritual obligation". In addition some seek to expand frenzied mathematical formulations and models to give a compelling justification of the expected phenomenon.[19,20,21]

---

[17] *Remaking Eden: How Genetic Engineering and Cloning Will Transform the American Family*, Lee M Silver, 1998.

[18] *Citizen Cyborg: Why Democratic Societies Must Respond to The Redesigned Human of the Future*, James Hughes, Cambridge MA, 2004.

[19] "An overview of models of technological singularity", Anders Sandberg in *The Transhumanist Reader*.

[20] *Mindsteps to the Cosmos*, Gerald Hawkins, World Scientific, 2002.

[21] "Simple equations for Vinge's technological singularity", Hans Moravec, February 1999. Available at: https://frc.ri.cmu.edu/~hpm/project.archive/robot.papers/1999/singularity.html

To conclude this showdown on the Man versus the Men it may be said again that being super-intelligent does not mean being super-powerful; "the speed and the viscosity of the rest of the world will limit physical and organizational changes ... physical changes will take time" (Max More).[22]

---

[22] "Singularity meets economy", Max More in *The Transhumanist Reader*.

Chapter Nine

Robots & Co.

Robots are clearly at the very center of the main concerns of the Transhumanists, all the more so as AI begins to give these mechanics a sort of mind (not yet to say a soul!). The field of the corresponding new science of "Robotics" keeps growing with a huge diversity of applications from the simplest ones to much elaborated developments close to very disturbing human similarities. Robots are now everywhere, at home, at the factory, in the hospital, at the operating room, even in the high space or deep in the seas! They are the 2.0 version of what was then known as the "automatons" or watchmaking. Such an extensive field makes it quite tricky to be exhaustively covered in a handful of pages.

The field of robotics is so scattered that this chapter will not be structured in sub-chapters as usual but in simple paragraphs in order to cover the subject in detail. This may also explain some redundancies to occur in the comments.

The only competitor of "mineral" robotics remains Genetic Editing in the biological field. It is not unlikely that humans may create an advanced sapiens being or artificial creature in a very near future. This without taking into account the opportunity to smarten ourselves up with added limbs or eyes as the Chinese have suggested with their embryonic research. This leads to the appropriate issue developed by some transhumanists, namely: "How smart does a brain have to be before it's *no longer* human?"

So there would be an intermediate world of mixed beings bringing together the particular performances of both the mechanical and the living world. As Zoltan Istvan[1] puts it: "Ultimately my hope is that pressure will be put on the United Nations to amend its own historic the Universal Declaration of Human Rights to include machine intelligences, cyborgs, advanced sapient beings, and even virtual persons. To not do so soon will show we have learned little from the tumultuous civil right era."

The start of the introduction of a smart "intelligence" in the machines will mark an important step forward from the old world of pure automatons, regulators, and other such purely mechanical devices.

1. Artificial Intelligence

Today robots are indissociable from the corresponding Artificial Intelligence. New tech products extensively use these recent opportunities, especially the robots. Let us recall the words of David Mindell,[2] a Massachusetts Institute of Technology (MIT) professor: "You can say that autonomy is the artificial intelligence that might live inside a robot. A.I. is kind of a loaded term. There has been a lot of debate around it for a long time. I use 'autonomy' because it's the word that people in robotics use these days. And I don't make the argument about intelligence, per se. There's a long history and interesting debate about intelligence. The full autonomy problem is an easier problem. It just doesn't work in a social context. The robot is very good at mapping, collecting data, and those are all tremendous engineering accomplishments."

David A. Mindell sees it as a largely positive development in our present 2.0 world whereas many are troubled with such an intrusion of the machines in our private sphere or in the workplace. Apart from the robots largely used in the factories there are now many applications close to the individual: driverless cars, Internet of Things, drone delivery, automated cashes and others also exotic, not to mention smartphones that conduct our daily life. All of that goes with a corresponding "intelligence" which

---

[1] "Rights in a post-Human world", Zoltan Istvan, 2018. Available at: https://www.cato-unbound.org/2018/04/13/zoltan-istvan/becoming-transhuman-complicated-future-robot-advanced-sapient-rights

[2] *Our Robots, Ourselves: Robotics and the Myths of Autonomy,* David A Mindell, Viking, 2015.

makes the objects genuine partners we sometimes hesitate to consider as really friendly.

Isaac Asimov outlined the Three Laws of Robotics in his famous 1950 science fiction classic, *I, Robot*. These were designed to protect humanity against their possible robotic creations. The most important was the first law: "A robot may not injure a human being or, through inaction, allow a human being to come to harm." Over 60 years later, a variety of U.S. military robots of various shapes and sizes — such as the Reaper drone — are now engineered to directly violate Asimov's law. For Peter Singer, this means "humans' 5000-year-old monopoly over the fighting of war is over".[3]

On the face of it robots can typically be defined as a computer-programmable machine capable of automatic actions. This encompasses a range of artificial devices out of the classical domain of the industrial robots that work in factory floors across the planet. For the United States Deputy Secretary of Defense Robert O. Work:[4] "The robot age thus confronts militaries, politicians, scholars, scientists, and activists with deep questions about the future of warfare, and even our humanity."

Robots are of first concern for transhumanists. Transhumanism is both a movement and belief that human should use technology and science to redesign ourselves beyond the limits of our biological constraints. This includes pure artificial creation of "intelligent autonomous objects". It is beginning to seem inevitable, though whether that's a good thing remains up for debate.

Every new serendipity arising in the huge field of Robotics causes a buzz. All this passes initially by an extended crunching of data that could be used as a deep memory by the AI of the machines. Then reinforcement and deep learning can be used to train algorithmic neural networks configured in independent layers which can be interconnected with nodes to help calculation take place. The computers are able to sift through mountains of data. They provide the robots with minute details and so give the

---

[3] *Ethics Into Action*, Peter Singer, Rowan & Littlefield, 2000 Revised ed.
[4] *Preparing for War in the Robotic Age*, Robert O. Work and Shawn Brimley, Center for a New American Security, 2014. Available at: https://s3.amazonaws.com/files.cnas.org/documents/CNAS_20YY_WorkBrimley.pdf

robot its life. In many situations such dedicated applications make the robot faster than a human.

The final goal of the robots is to be so versatile as to copy the human capacity in as many situations as a human might face in his diversity. This "Holy Grail" might manifest in a human-like machine able to challenge both the human intelligence and the human muscles. This would prefigure the Great Replacement beloved by Transhumanists.

2. Robots at Work

Robots, in general, are keen on outperforming humans in many situations where precision,[5] reliability, strength, fatigue resistance, and repeatability are the key requirements. They also benefit from other significant advantages of never being tired, never sleeping, never getting afraid, never stopping for lunch, never going on strike, and so forth … The most drastic downsides of these perks are that they are not (so) able to behave autonomously, they need a human intelligence behind. Robots do not eat anything but nevertheless require enough energy (most of the time this means electricity).

They adore crunching big data on the Cloud and talking with computers to the point that a dedicated network has been created (Robot Earth from Google) to allow robots to directly exchange their experiences and data. Their binary language fundamentally obeys a rigorous Boolean logic even if "fuzzy logic" can bring a little flexibility to their decision processes. "Formal logic" is also used to check the absence of bugs in the software (Safety Integrity Level).

Doron Zeilberger, an Israelian mathematician said that: "The computer logic is bound to exceed our conceptual understanding". The complexity will soon be too large for our human brain which already fails even in some simple situations. It still remains to be answered: how to check if the computer is right or if it crashed somewhere?

Robots, yesterday, were rather simple machines used in factories; they have now entered our daily lives; they dislike letting you drive your car on

---

[5]This is especially essential in some applications such as high resolution Integrated Circuits fabrication or surgery. We are at the diffraction limit of the human or optical vision.

your own, or making comments about nothing in a speech synthesis. They are able to see your face and know everything about your feelings almost like a human could do. It has been expected that: "An estimated 120 million cars will be equipped with voice-recognition systems next year, up to 40 million in 2018."[6] So robots will soon become personal assistants able to help the "not improved man" in any circumstance!

Facebook has developed three projects in order to allow robots to understand on their own through their experience rather than through data prepared in advance:

1. A six legged robot is learning how to walk by itself.
2. It induced some curiosity in the learning process.
3. It learned how to use a haptic detection (touch) of the environment.

The Japanese roboticist Masahiro Mori is concerned with humanoid robots: he states that the external resemblance of the machine with a real human will generate an uncomfortable feeling of unease. The more the resemblance is acute the more the observed artificial details will be striking and dissonant.

That is the reason why "social robots" do not seek to show a perfect likeness but clearly display their artificiality and even adopt a childish character such as a toy appearance. In relations with robots there is an influence of the robot behavior on the human partner who may feel proximity and a tendency to do the same thing through the robot by behaving accordingly with the machine.

However various issues can be formulated concerning the possibility of identifying a robot (as sophisticated as we could imagine) with a human: people are now asking the question of granting legal and moral status to an object which does not exhibit any consciousness or inwardness. There is an underlying idea that as long as the robot does not display any subjectivity, there is no discussion of granting the robot any rights. If, one day, a subjectivity could be attributed to robots that will occur in a different way on the basis of their own channels to learn the ways of the world and decode it conveniently.

---

[6]"The spy inside your car", Jaclyn Trop, *Fortune*, January 1, 2019.

Indeed there are already precedents for that. We know that Saudi Arabia granted the robot Sophia a citizenship, whereas the "virtual" robot Mirai got the residency status of Tokyoite, but could be considered as purely anecdotic. The Legal Affairs Division of the European Commission for the robotics is considering the possibility of a creation of a dedicated status for "electronic persons" and their associated responsibilities.

The relationship between man and machine has become so pregnant that a new term has been dedicated to this coupling: the Cobotic. This domain is trans-disciplinary, at the interface between cognition, biomechanics, and pure robotics. It mainly applies to industrial activity but may extend to many other sectors. The limit of these issues reach the situation of the "augmented" man.

The Cobot or Robot Assistant[7] differs from the classical robot by virtue of not being autonomous[8] (passive device). Medical robots are essentially Cobots because of the necessary human supervision.

2.1. *Industry*

Charlie Chaplin[9] was a visionary of the modern era when it came to the domination of machines. He forecasted the repetitive tasks of the production lines but, at that time, did not imagine that machines themselves could, one day to come, replace men for these harsh works.

Robots have come to deliver the workers from such tedious tasks. Workshops, triage areas, and any place where repetitive works are required, have become the exclusive domain of tireless robots.

This has led to a shortage of jobs in these fields, but other opportunities arise with the development of the technologies (for instance, robot fabrication) which require new skills and knowledges. Men and women workers are in the same boat. Forecasters of the World Economic Forum[10]

---

[7] "Cobots for the automobile assembly line", Prasad Akella, *Proceedings of the IEEE International Conference on Robotics and Automation*, 1999.

[8] "Cobots", Michael Peshkin and J. Edward Colgate, *Industrial Robots*, 26(5), 335–341, 1999.

[9] *Modern Times*, Charlie Chaplin, 1936 (film).

[10] *The Future of Jobs Report 2018*, World Economic Forum, 17 September 2018. Available at: https://www.weforum.org/reports/the-future-of-jobs-report-2018

state in 2018 that within five years the robotic revolution shall create 58 million more jobs; thus inducing a rupture in the world of work.[11]

That induced Bill Gates to worry that: "would the robot that stole a job have to pay charges." He is not the only one to raise the question … many governments are already looking for such new resources!

The World Economic Forum also anticipates that 54% of the employees of the big companies will need a permanent recycling of their competences. This is already noticeable in California with the Z generation who are more likely attracted by a hiring in a company proposing such an enhancement program in new technologies, than in a big and renowned company, as was the case before.

Of course, extreme environments have been sites of great progress in our use of robots. They have forced us to adopt robotics, 10, 20, 30 years before some of the more ordinary environments, simply out of necessity.

Space exploration, as well as the deep ocean, requires artificial means to investigate the remote environment. There is no other way to explore Mars right now. Even with the New Horizon's Mission to Pluto that was in the news this summer, you can see the human contact for these autonomous robots and how the autonomy is shot through with human design and intention. If it's true for space, it is going to be just as true in a factory, or on a highway, or in an operating room where there are a lot more people physically around. We shall deal with robots in space later in more details.

The automobile industry is especially eager to put robots at work in every stage of the production plant: they transport, assemble parts, weld or stick others in an uninterrupted process. However, they would not be able to face any unforeseen incident such as, for instance, the presence of a moth in the painting tunnel; no doubt that the moth will be painted too on the car body!

2.2. Energy

Energy is not a favored topic for the transhumanist philosophers, possibly because it is a trivial, material contingency only the concern of basic technologists?

---

[11] According to Bank of America Merrill Lynch and Bank of England.

From the most remote times Man has always looked for a more comfortable life and consequently created new, constraining, and inescapable needs. This lasted as a priority from the mastering of the art of fire to the present status of the Anthropocene. Each time a new source of energy has been discovered and developed, a new civilization has emerged.

So we crossed successively the Bronze Age, the Iron one, the steam machine epoch, the electricity era, and we are now in the nuclear age; nothing new happened to start a new 2.0 civilization but we still are consuming the resources that Nature provides us. Transhumanists are not so vocal on the subject but there is a fundamental lack.

Energy is a virtual concept directly related to life, whether biological or artificial. Living species take their energy from combining food and Oxygen thus giving bio-chemical exo-energetic reactions; energy is a transitory state resulting from a reaction of a potential source which is obtained after a succession of transformations and many consecutive losses. It is possible to juggle energy but in no way create energy from nothing.

Regarding the robots the only need is electricity (from batteries in the smartphones to solar cells in the satellites or to power stations in the data centers). But electricity cannot be found in natural fields, it has to be produced following complex ways before being used. Currently the most efficient solution to provide us with massive electrical energy is unquestionably the nuclear sources and their steam machines (as before!). Like it or not, there is a global bulimia of MWh constantly reflated by a growing global population!

Transhumanists mostly support the development of nuclear energy and its extension to fusion reaction which could lead to safer plants and "cleaner" energy as proposed by the ITER[12] project.

Unfortunately energy is not able to be conveniently stored; the most easy and largely used solution relies on chemical batteries but this is up to now of a limited but crucial efficiency restricted to specific applications.

Robots, wherever they could be, fully depend on electricity and this may be the more severe restriction to their usage, especially when dealing with distant operations such as in the space. Data centers are especially

---

[12] International Thermonuclear Experimental Reactor.

electricity-intensive and the biggest ones are installed close to a strong power station in order to limit losses.

2.3. *Military applications*

The domain of weapons has for a long time been a privileged field for robots[13] and war machinery. One of the essential aims is to improve biologically or artificially the capacities of the soldier in the army,[14] for instance enhancing night vision or the capacity to resist falling asleep. At present, the solution remains to bluntly replace the vulnerable human combatant with a machine (as intelligent and effective when possible). Many attempts were made to design two flat-footed robots to be able to be as agile as a man could be, but the technical complexity of the bipedal displacement did not lead to satisfying results and it is, here too, chosen to proceed with wheels or articulated arms solutions devoid of any humanoid likeness. These devices are very useful in especially dangerous operations such as mine detection and neutralization.

These robots are more largely used in the battlefield with unmanned systems (such as in the war in Iraq or Afghanistan which has become "largely robotics" as an officer put it). For instance the PackBot is, as it is described: "the size of a lawn mower, it mounts all sorts of cameras and sensors, as well as a nimble arm with four joints. It moves using four 'flippers'. These are tiny treads that can also rotate on an axis, allowing the robot not only to roll forward and backward using the treads as a tank would, but also to flip its tracks up and down (almost like a seal moving) to climb stairs, rumble over rocks, squeeze down twisting tunnels, and even swim underwater. The cost to the United States of this 'death' was $150,000."

Such devices are very efficient against the Improvised Explosive Devices (IED) and any "Three D's" tasks that are dull, dirty, or dangerous. As an officer puts it: "when a robot dies, you don't have to write a letter to its mother."

---

[13] *Wired for War: The Robotics Revolution and Conflict in the 21st Century*, P. W. Singer, The Penguin Press, 2009.

[14] Roco and Bainbridge, *Converging Technologies*.

The world of unmanned systems at war is not confined to the ground. Cruise missiles are autonomous flying bombs able to navigate on their own at low altitude and supersonic speed in order to deliver their warhead over long distances and with a high precision. This is purely robotics!

They now face competition with other Unmanned Aerial Vehicles which are cheaper and easier to operate in many circumstances: the drones which, more or less, resemble a conventional plane; it flies at low speed but can look for its prey 24 hours nonstop at a height of 26,000 feet. This flying robot is in no way autonomous but is flown through the "remote-split" operation of a human pilot who can stay 7,500 miles away of the war zone. The connection is provided through satellites from a set of converted single-wide trailers located mostly at Nellis and Creech Air Force bases in Nevada.

Such operations have created the novel situation of pilots experiencing the psychological disconnect of being "at war" while still dealing with the pressures of home. In the words of one Predator pilot, "[y]ou see Americans killed in front of your eyes and then have to go to a PTA meeting." Says another, "[y]ou are going to war for 12 hours, shooting weapons at targets, directing kills on enemy combatants, and then you get in the car, drive home, and within 20 minutes you are sitting at the dinner table talking to your kids about their homework."

In other applications DARPA (Defense Advanced Research Projects Agency) is developing a man/machine interface with an augmented reality in a helmet (Hololens) which is able to manage direct control by thought of any active system of cyber defense or even a swarm of unmanned aerial vehicles.

In spite of these multiple inconveniences it must be remarked that the computer, when controlling a fighter aircraft can easily surpass the maneuvering capability of a human. A recent air combat was organized in a simulator assembly between a dedicated computer[15] and a Top Gun experienced pilot. The winner was indisputably the machine and the pilot gave this comment: "I had the uncomfortable feeling that the machine knew in advance what I was going to do!" On top of that a fully robotized

---

[15] The computer was a mini one, the size of a smartphone yet able to set up a fight strategy 250 times faster than a human!

fighter can better withstand harsher flight conditions such as high accelerations or sharp maneuvers above 10 g that a human pilot could not.

3. Robots in Society

Robots play and will play an increasing role in our societies as time goes by and as their intelligence improves. It can be expected that they will leach into every corner of our organizations.

In the U.S., the court's expert cabinet BakerHostetler hired a digital judge (elaborated from the famous multipurpose IBM Watson), which replaces fifty lawyers! And, following Ray Kurzweil, the U.S. and Europe will adopt laws regulating the relations between individuals and robots; this will take place by 2022! These new laws will formalize the rights, the duties and other legal restrictions and related responsibilities for the robots.

In 2017, a vote took place at the European Parliament.[16] The debate is prepared following the report of Mady Delvaux who prescribes the creation of a specific legal personality of robots in particular on the grounds that the most sophisticated autonomous robots are able, at present, to take "autonomous decisions in a judicious manner" or interact "in an independent way with a third party". It should be considered that there is in any case the will of a man or an organization behind any robot, even autonomous.

One might even go a step further in the field of intelligent robots: some emphasize to anticipate criminal acts from a deep data analysis of the individual behaviors considered to be "risky". Chinese and Japanese already experiment with such "previsionist" softwares operating from huge data bases of personal data, whereas some are already at work in Chicago, London, or Munich. Of course this is an open door for a larger utilization such as hunting a political opponent or terrorist.

Algorithms are able to crunch mountains of data to find individuals prone to becoming involved in wrongdoing before they happen. This could be especially important in the situations where terrorism rages (as the CIA

---

[16]"Parlement Européen: Faire Des Robots L'égal des Hommes?", *Généthique*, January 20, 2017. Available at: http://www.genethique.org/fr/parlement-europeen-faire-des-robots-legal-des-hommes-66896.html#.XQ45h41lLRZ

emphasized). A dedicated company (Palantir) has been founded by Peter Thiel (from PayPal) but all of that raises many wide ethical issues not readily identifiable. This brings to mind the "electronic democracy" suggested by Isaac Asimov.[17]

Chinese are largely involved in robotics and namely AI. Significant investments have been carried out to promote electronic chips or electric cars for example. For Kai-Fu Lee,[18] a Taiwanese venture capitalist there are four decisive factors Chinese now have:

- A huge data base concerning the individuals or the masses: facial recognition, behaviors, habits (even for pupils in their classrooms!). Some companies are well known in the market such as SenseTime or Face++.
- Hungry and reactive entrepreneurs.
- Large expertise in AI and in the technology of the detection of emotional factors of employees, from face recognition.
- Attentive directives and investments from the Chinese government for STEM.[19] The defeat of Chinese Go champion Ke Jie by the computer Alpha Go (Deep Mind) has been a real trigger!

The Japanese are especially fond of robots, namely the humanoid ones; that strongly prefigures a possible close cohabitation: Kodomoroid and Otomaroid are charming hostesses that (who?) welcome the public at the Emerging Sciences Museum of Tokyo and politely answer your questions in Japanese or English language. Some said that Komodoroid even asked the TV to invite it (her?) to give a show!

They even made the robot contribute to religious services; this is cheaper than a conventional ceremony and provides a solution to the problem of professional shortage. Some examples follow:

1. Pepper, the robot, sings Buddhist prayers and mantras and can be rented for participating at ceremonies such as weddings or funerals. It

---

[17] *Franchise*, Isaac Asimov, Quinn Publishing, 1955.

[18] *AI Superpowers: China, Silicon Valley, and the New World Order*, Kai-Fu Lee, Houghton Mifflin Harcourt, 2018.

[19] Science, Technology, Engineering, Mathematics.

is well disposed for passing the hat to collect money and beat the drum as the tradition requires!

2. Buddhist or Shintoists also accept to follow the religious service of a priest-robot and give the replies in a common prayer. The AI helps the machine to fully behave like a human priest.

3. Recently a Buddhist funeral ceremony had been celebrated in Japan to commemorate the disassembling of 114 AIBO robots which were out of duty! Recovered parts would be reused.

4. Robots and the Arts

Robots are not yet spontaneously sensitive to art but they begin to understand it to the point that they are able to imitate a fabulous painter so much so that experts were fascinated. On April 5, 2016 a computer was programmed to analyze the way Rembrandt achieved his painting technic and it was then allowed to improvise a portrait, using a 3D printer, to simulate the brush stroke of the now deceased artist. The work was out of the "inspiration" of the machine which was kept "free", following some limited guidelines to keep in agreement with the epoch. So, Rembrandt was in some way resuscitated by a machine.[20]

It is well known that Van Gogh (nobody knows exactly why but some said he might have been helped by Gauguin?!), one day, decided to cut his left ear and then make a painting of the result. The mitochondrial DNA of Van Gogh was recovered, sequenced, and cloned from an envelope that the painter used in 1883 and biologists grew the corresponding cells given by a descendent to achieve an exact reconstruction of the lost ear through a 3D robot printer. No doubt it was exactly a copy of HIS ear!

5. Robots and Medicine

Medicine is so large a field for robots that we just limit the discussion to the more apparent applications. Obviously this field is especially favored by the transhumanists who foresee a wonderful future to come soon.

---

[20] https://www.nextrembrandt.com/

Here is a short list of the many opportunities now available:

1. First may be the intelligent diagnostic robots that are now beginning to extract from the medical data they accumulate every day; the diagnostic arises from the statistical comparison of countless similar cases and an intelligent appraisal. This is more rigorous than the limited human view of a physician but also less intuitive. This automatic diagnostic will likely play an increasing role in medicine and sooner or later a dialogue will prevail between doctors, however competent they may be, and a more and more indispensable robot. Psychiatry and epidemiology especially strongly support robot assistance or (with time) a purely independent operation.

2. In the future, this ubiquity of the robots will also deeply affect the pharmaceutical industry (drug fabrication as well as their delivery) which has to become more personalized and diversified with the onset of predictive medicine that prevents the onset of diseases by evaluating a probability.

3. Another domain where robots are precious is that of biological analysis: this refers to traditional blood, urine, or biopsy analysis but also more elaborate researches such as the automatic sequencing of DNA which is now routinely operated at a reduced cost.

4. Surgery already favors robot assistance, mainly because of the high precision and reliability a machine is able to provide. Obviously the robot is mostly tethered to a human but in some situations it could be free to take decisions and act.

The first fully operational dentist robot can be found in China.[21] It undergoes delicate implant operations. The commentator added: "Robots can safely conduct dental surgeries like implantations with more accuracy and agility in a narrow space like oral cavity". Also, Yomi, a robot system designed to assist dentists in dental implant procedures was approved by the U.S. Food and Drug Administration (March 2019). This signals a good start to a move toward the reign of the robot in dentistry.

---

[21] "A Chinese robot has performed the world's first automated dental implant", Kevin Lui, *Time*, September 22, 2017. Available at: https://time.com/4952886/china-world-first-dental-surgery-robot-implant/

At the same time, in Berkeley,[22] an autonomous robot is allowed, on its own, to locate, identify, and cut cancerous tissues in well-defined limits.[23]

Many similar examples could be found in ears, eyes, or skull surgery every time high precision and reliability are required that exceed human performance:

- Impressive progress has been made by the intelligent imaging technologies to appropriately guide robots in delicate explorations of the human body in the fields of endoscopy, coelioscopy, not to mention ingestible nanorobots to explore the internal functioning of the digestive system (the battery of which is edible!).
- Telediagnostics and telemedicine allow remote assistance, which is especially appreciated in cases of emergency.
- Prosthetic limbs have seen substantial progresses in the form of exoskeletons, training bots, robotic nurses, or micro-robots for targeted therapy.

It is also worth mentioning a particular domain where robots play an increasing role at the cutting edge of the trend between medicine, individual comfort, or social needs: the sex robot. Depending on the place and circumstances, there could arise a very real need. This is already the case in many countries where sexual life is hampered by social or professional requirements.[24]

Sexbots are to increasingly exploit AI in order to move, speak, develop full facial animation, get adapted to the mood of the users,[25] and become real partners for everybody, not only ugly or handicapped people. These bots can be chosen for male or female use; some extension could be later emphasized to make them also able to clean the home, cook, or iron a shirt!

[22] "Humans are underrated", Geoff Calvin, *Fortune*, August 1, 2015.

[23] The automatic corrector tells me I have to say "his" in reference to the robot. As of now this robot is incorrect.

[24] "Meet the Activist Fighting Sex Robots", Andrea Morris, *Science*, September 26, 2018. Available at: https://www.forbes.com/sites/andreamorris/2018/09/26/meet-the-activist-fighting-sex-robots/

[25] "I, Sex Robot: The health implications of the sex robot industry", Chantal Cox-George and Susan Bewley, *BMJ Sexual and Reproductive Health*, 44, 153–154, 2018.

To quote literature: "An animated take on the sex doll. While this is not something that gets much coverage in the mainstream media, the market for such dolls is massive. People are willing to pay obscene amounts of money for top-class sex dolls and that money is driving even more development. The king of the hill when it comes to high-end sex dolls RealDoll X from the company Realbotix. Their products start at an eye-popping $6,000 and go up from there depending on your customizations and advanced features.

They've developed silicon skin that feels like the real thing. The doll's 'flesh' also has to feel right and you can even get heating to simulate body temperature or appreciate a vocal participation! Clearly RealDoll would not sell their product if it caused disgust in people, so they have gone to great lengths to make their products as real and friendly as possible. It may be surprising to a lot of people, but sex doll aficionados spend only some (if any) time doing anything sexual with their toy. For some lonely or otherwise atypical individuals, the doll is actually a companion, someone who sits at the dinner table and watches TV with you and so on."

One day the robots that will care for us and act as our helpers and companions may end up with quite a lot of sexbot DNA in them! Because while companies like Boston Dynamics try to make machines that can cater to our material needs, companies like RealDoll are working to make ones that cater to our emotional ones. In the end, our transhuman future is going to need both of these approaches to be worth it.

Then, to get closer to the Transhumanist "medicine", there is a very exploratory field which already gathers adepts: Cryonics.[26] Some organizations more or less related to transhumanism offer their services such as the Cryonics Institute that "provides an ambulance ride to the high-tech hospital of the future"! That means that a dead body can be frozen and indefinitely maintained at low temperature in the hope that, someday, an appropriate technology could bring back this body to life. A dedicated robot is in charge of the security of the cold chain.

---

[26] *Serons Nous Immortels*, Ray Kurzweil and Terry Grossman, Dunod Editions, 2006; *Au-delà de nos limites biologiques*, Miroslav Radman, Plon, 2011.

Finally, out of the field of real medicine it is worth mentioning a non-fictional[27] anticipation proposed by Mark O'Connell who "explores the staggering possibilities and moral quandaries that present themselves when you of think of your body as a device."

6. Robots at Home

Since more than a half century ago we became accustomed to robots at home and the corresponding comfort they brought in the households. Refrigerators, washing machines, air conditioners, television sets, and the like were everywhere and they were largely accepted.

We have entered the digital 2.0 era and things are changing. The computer has made our lives interrelated at a global level by taking part in our personal activities with the corresponding Internet. This has sharpened appetites for new companies which found a means to enter into our private sphere and make their business directly, permanently, and with costless machines.

The Internet of Things (IoT) put the home robots at work under provisional programing. It is mainly intended to keep the house in order when the residents are away: both husband and wife are at work and the kids (if any) at school; these are the modern usages.

Amazon Alexa is an intelligent personal assistant which works as a hub for every domestic device (alarms, vacuum cleaner, heating, air conditioning, microwave oven, and so on). It can even order a pizza or pass a list of orders to the supermarket. Alexa is also fully fluent to speak in many languages; it can prepare a programmed TV show or a "voice game"; it could also be able to hear your personal phone calls and that is very close to an intrusive way to spy.

That is so wide a competence field that it could not leave Google indifferent and its voracious appetite for data gathering has found here a real mine. Every exchange is dissected to feed a database which gathers everything about your personal intimate habits. We have entered an era of a kind of collective e-conviviality! Google knows everything about you even if it officially recommends to its employees: "don't be evil"!

---

[27] *To be a Machine*, Mark O'Connell, Granta Publications, 2017.

To conclude with robots at home and transhumanism it is worth mentioning fiction shows such as TV series, games, role-plays, comics largely displayed on the TV channels.

7. The Transhumanist Philosophy of Robotics

The idea to create intelligent artificial "beings" as proposed by Hans Moravec[28] strongly influenced the development of the transhumanism philosophy.

It was suggested as an interdisciplinary approach to understand and evaluate the possibilities to surpass the biological limits. Futurology and various domains of ethics are studied including a "robot ethics". In the view of such a utilitarian philosophy, the natural could be at worst considered an obstacle to any progress.

Many people trust in the compatibility between the human spirit and the hardware/software of equipment; they are confident in a future possibility of transferring human consciousness into alternative media in a kind of mind downloading. Nevertheless, some such as the Neo-luddites[29] are definitely opposed to any replacement of human workers by machines, even sophisticated ones.

Some are afraid of a foreseeable society by 2050 which could be dominated by hyper-performing individuals (machine, cyborgs, or improved humans as well) which could leave out the others "minus".

This was pessimistically viewed by Georges Bernanos when he said that "there is always more to be gained with satisfying the human vices than the real needs".

---

[28] "When will computer hardware match the human brain?", Hans Moravec, *Journal of Evolution and Technology*, 1, 1998.
[29] "Technologies of self-perfection", James Hughes, September 20, 2004. Available at: https://ieet.org/index.php/IEET2/more/hughes20040922

Chapter Ten

What About Space and the Post-Human Realm?

In this chapter we will be ineluctably tempted to get close to science fiction. Transhumanists are attracted by the mysteries of space, especially remote spaces that have yet to be discovered. They anticipate that space is to play a key role in the future of humanity, which is now on the verge of a big leap. What is to be taken as plausible?

Most transhumanists are very pro-space for a variety of reasons but it is not clear if the real motivation is to conquer space (out of sheer scientific curiosity, gaining resources, exploring the Earth from above and organizing global communications) or to escape an Earth that has become unduly unfriendly (due to overpopulation, resource depletion, nuclear or other wars).

These basic questions that has haunted humanity for eternity: are we alone in this universe? Could there be, elsewhere, some other kinds of life? Would they have solved the issue of the extended duration of the galactic travels? Is our universe part of a larger set of a multi-universe? Would science be able to bring some light in the stream of the transhumanist (or posthumanist) thinking? A more distant philosophical preoccupation attempts to answer.

1. Space Is A Recent Issue

The sky and its mysteries have long been a matter of curiosity, imagination, observation, and even fear for humans. This unfathomable enigma gives rise to the question of knowing where all of this comes from and whether there is a hidden will behind. There has been, for millennia, the irrepressible desire to know.

Men could not, until recently, approach the issue otherwise than gazing at the sky in a starry night. Even with telescopes our knowledge remained limited. Short of being able to physically go outside the atmosphere; we are stuck on the Earth! Man was not programmed to leave his birth land ... but that did not stop him from trying!

But we have to remember that accessible ultimate technology, fundamental questionings, and futuristic imagination can only meet in the space consideration, outside our conventional world.

1.1. *Near space and remote space*

Dealing with transhumanists in particular, the discussions are rich in projections toward a possible future. Space is a rather hostile and dangerous environment because of the vacuum conditions, the hazardous level of radiations, the zero gravity, and other awkward parameters.

But for a half century things have profoundly changed with the achievement of rockets that enabled men and material to venture out of the Earth's atmosphere. This challenge is shared between robots and some audacious astronauts. In a rather short while, fabulous work has already been accomplished but the subject is so huge and the prospects so unrestricted that I must say that we still are at the very beginning of the story.

Currently, space can be approached in three layers:

1. The Classical layer easily (?) reachable for a human presence, up to 300 or 400 kilometers (km) from the ground (possible to be extended to 20,000–30,000 km for satellites to be "stationary"). Such a presence could not be upheld without the permanent support of robots. This is the place where a multitude of fully automatic satellites crowd to give us weather predictions, global positioning, detailed earth images, global communications, and so on. There are even space stations that provide humans the possibility of an extended stay in space and allow acclimatization to the special conditions of zero gravity in the medium term.

Until the historical success of Sputnik and its "bip-bip", on October 4, 1957, the launches of satellites of Earth never stopped. This "Earth suburb" is now crowded with countless robots from many nations and even, now, private companies. It has become a new battlefield for major economic issues and there is speculation of a future business in tourist trade. These satellites, at the beginning, were rather complex, big, and heavy but the trend now is rather to multiply less expensive "nano satellites" dedicated to well-focused functions albeit with limited livespan. New Integrated Circuits and softwares allow much more compact and light architectures.

A nanosatellite (or CubeSats) revolution is coming: a new wave of colonization is being carried out by small, fast, and inexpensive systems that are enabling companies that need space in order to reach their objectives and expand their services to gain a foothold in this area. In 2017, more than 300 nanosatellites were launched into space and by 2022 up to 75% of all nanosatellites are forecast to be in orbit for commercial reasons.

2. A more remote intermediate layer is represented by the Moon which has already accommodated the presence of a handful of human explorers after the historical trip of Neil Armstrong in 1969. There are plenty of autonomous robots scouting out the place, even on the hidden dark face. The interest over the Moon vanished after a period of great and exciting activity. However, recently interest was again raised with the prospect of using the Moon as a fixed base to look at the Earth or as a springboard toward the far space human exploration. Yet, the resources available on the Moon presently seem limited and of an unprofitable exploitation.

3. A far remote and infinitely extended space in the galaxy or even further. This is, at the moment very exploratory, and the prospect of a human presence close to transhumanist utopia (unless...). The main advancement of our knowledge of this far remote limit of the universe still remains in the domain of large telescopes which provide us with such huge amounts of data that they require a lot of time to be managed. Some long range probes have nevertheless been sent beyond the Sun and keep sending their electro-magnetic messages in spite of the enormous distance they have already covered.

1.2. *The interest in space technologies is not for nothing*

Undoubtedly, the intellectual interest in knowing more about our external environment is a major goal but this gratuitous eagerness has to be supported economically. Most of them (and corresponding fundings) are, directly or not, motivated by military goals.

However, communications are also an area of active business and developments. The GPS[1] allows locating of connected beacons (such as smartphones) with a precision in the range of 3 to 50 meters on Earth. The challenger is currently the European Galileo (some 30 satellites of the EAS[2] at 23,222 km from the Earth) which will be able to reach a precision of 3 meters. Also to be mentioned are the Russian Glonass and the Chinese Beidou active in the sky.

Now, more than ever, space is seen as a commercial enterprise. Large, medium-sized, and start-up businesses are all heading towards the final business frontier. Hundreds of start-ups are benefiting from the savings involved in the new nanosatellite constellations. Furthermore, the nature of this system means that the loss of one nanosatellite would not be catastrophic, as the service would remain active thanks to the rest of the constellation.

CubSats are expected to play a key role in the development of the IoT at home, in autonomous transport operations, or in traffic monitoring. They provide smart support to the Robot Earth network which interconnects robots on Earth. Not to mention a wealth of other applications such as crop controls, local meteorology, or giving key insight into the city's economic activity. The field is unlimited!

This has come to a point where the space close to the Earth begins to be filled with operating or dead satellites, debris, and the like; it is becoming polluted not unlike plastics in the seas.

1.3. *Moon as a starting place*

NASA[3] is looking for better knowledge of the Moon in order to establish a sustained human presence there. They initiated a plan to send a dozen payloads to the Moon. Thomas Zurbuchen, NASA administrator in Washington,

---

[1] Global Positioning System.

[2] European Space Agency.

[3] National Aeronautics and Space Administration.

shared that: "Each demonstrates either a new science instrument or a technological innovation that supports scientific and human exploration objectives, and many have broader applications for Mars and beyond."

One of the aims of such scouting experiments is to get a better knowledge of the lunar terrain: temperature in depth, electromagnetic activity, and Moondust (lunar regolith) as well as the influence of solar winds. Equipment for a prolonged stay on the Moon is expected to follow soon. All of that precludes the next giant step of a future mission to Mars. A preliminary mission objective is already set to place in orbit the Trace Gas Orbiter in order to hunt for methane or other organic compounds in its atmosphere.

The Americans are not alone in the race to the Moon; Russians are also active as well as China, Japan, Israel, and more recently India (who, incidentally, would have discovered the presence of water molecules and ice on the Moon).[4]

1.4. *The future of space*

Aside from the human or robot investigations and travels it is worth mentioning the permanent exploration of the far limit of our universe through the direct imaging through telescopes. This leads us to the universe's past, close to the Big Bang origin of the planetary systems.

This research was operated at the same time from the ground of the Earth and also from space in order to investigate the potential for life in the planetary systems.

In the former case, a flurry of new telescopes have blossomed, up to 39 meters in diameter, in Hawaii at 4,200 meters altitude using "adaptive optics"; other projects yet more ambitious are on track. Not forgetting the largest radio-telescope in the word (some 500 meters in diameter) which is under completion in China; it is currently considered as a better chance to detect extraterrestrial beings.

In the latter case the Hubble Space Telescope (HST) provided us for years with astonishing images of the stars in the range of the extended visible spectrum and now the new JWST[5] is to bring a new vision of the celestial bodies from the "Lagrangian point 2" where it is planned to orbit.

---

[4] https://en.wikipedia.org/wiki/Lunar_water.
[5] James West Space Telescope.

Also, radio-telescopes have been combined in a global network electronically connected in real time and covering the five continents (VLBI[6] network) to successfully achieve a high resolution and prove the existence of a narrow stream of matter emerging from a gravitational wave involving two neutron stars. The phenomenon happened in a galaxy some 130 million light years away and corresponding delay in the remote past, closer to the Big Bang.

2. Space Travels and Colonization

Space is a much appreciated field of thought for the transhumanists, the only limit of which stays in science fiction. In this way we would require a super-intelligence and Elon Musk[7] said that "humans must merge with machines to enhance our own intellect"!

As Istvan Zoltan (a famous transhumanist) puts it: "As we enter the transhumanist age … space exploration might once again dramatically lead us forward in discovering the most our species can become." But "new ways of sleeping, recycling breathable air and preserving foods and drink would likely have to be developed." In the same way, he added: "the newly written Transhumanist Bill of Rights has a mandate for space exploration as one of its key six points."

The onward exploration of planets, comets, or asteroids: this remains (still for the moment) the exclusive domain of the unmanned robots even if daring projects are elaborated for a Mars "terraforming".

Currently our Earth is the only example of a life-bearing world, so astronomers search for similar environments in case we would need to migrate out of it. These conditions for finding a convenient "habitability" are not easily fulfilled: size of the planet, atmosphere, and magnetic field to get rid of radiations, presence of water, right distance from a "Sun", temperature, and so on. We might have to accept less ideal conditions and adapt to the requirements of nature.

---

[6] Very Long Baseline Interferometry.

[7] "No death and an enhanced life: Is the future transhuman?", Robin McKie, *Guardian*, May 6, 2018. Available at: https://www.theguardian.com/technology/2018/may/06/no-death-and-an-enhanced-life-is-the-future-transhuman

That does not prevent exploring and exploiting these uncomfortable planets, comets, or asteroids and looking for precious minerals. In 1970 the probe Venera 7 was the first interplanetary successful attempt, reaching Venus and transmitting data until crashing. In 1971 Mars 3 was the first to succeed in soft landing on Mars. These are examples of the preliminary missions to get into contact with remote planets using robotic spacecrafts.

To go further with a human mission, a key issue remains to shorten the travel's delays which often appear prohibitive. Many exotic solutions are proposed, from a special conditioning of the astronaut to electron propelled vehicles. In a further prospect (Mark Zuckerberg of the Breakthrough Initiative)[8] it was suggested to launch "a tiny light sail spacecraft called StarChips on a 4.37 light year-journey to Alpha Centauri at 15–20 per cent of the speed of light using lasers on Earth".

Then there were the farthest human made probes Voyager 1 and 2 that explored space beyond the Sun, outside the heliosphere, some 30,000 billion km away and were able to send reliable messages. Voyager 2 motors were recently restarted, 37 years after the launch, to change the route.

Concerning a possible extraterrestrial colonization or settlement, many arguments (pro and con) have been expressed, namely in favor, by transhumanists.[9] No space colony has been built so far and that is estimated to present a set of huge technological as well as economic challenges but a considerable number of advocates (such as Freeman Dyson or even Stephen Hawking) for such space settlements in these very hostile environments have spoken out[10] (loudly), arguing that within a couple of centuries we will face the prospect of an extinction of our species (taking into account the limitations of our growth).

Some pretend that enormous resources in materials and energy lie in space, not to speak of the "simple" asteroid mining. They said that

---

[8] https://breakthroughinitiatives.org/board

[9] "Astronomical waste: The opportunity cost of delayed technological development", Nick Bostrom, *Utilitas*, 15(3), 2003.

[10] "The top three reasons to colonize space", Robert Roy Britt, October 8, 2001; "Stephen Hawking: Humanity Must Colonize Space to Survive", Tariq Malik, *Space.com*, April 13, 2013.

harnessing these resources can lead to much economic development.[11] To achieve this potential target a celestial body must satisfy four requirements to overcome the exorbitant costs of the mission:

1. Enough data confirming the presence of these resources.
2. Reasonable orbital parameters for accessibility.
3. Feasible technical concepts for mining.
4. A positive net economic estimation.

It will then be left to demonstrate that these resources could become available with better technology and improved value of space economy.

2.1. Terraforming

Why is there such a panic and urgency to leave Earth?

There are two possible reasons: the first is the increasing level of global population which is compounded by the increasing life expectation (so promoted by the transhumanists). The second one is the worrying decrease of the available natural resources (oil, minerals, water, and so on) which, in the long run will, assuredly, become problematic.

Meanwhile governments and non-governmental organizations together ceaselessly invent new reasons of concerns (more or less justified) at a global scale: global warming, CO_2 emission, water-use restrictions, weather deregulation, etc... All of that pleads in favor of a quest for a convenient lifeboat available for a space-transfer in case of emergency!

Following the technologist ideas, transhumanists evoked the possibility of future generations leaving the Earth and colonizing another planet, with the possibility of changing their human constitution to make it compatible with a drastically different environment. To travel and survive in the deep space the Man would have to be small, radiation-hardened, or even at the embryonic state![12]

---

[11] "Mars colonization: Technically feasible, affordable, and a universal human drive", Thomas O Paine, Economic Development National Forum, 1992.

[12] Somewhat close to the "little green men"!

If we ever want to achieve things like terraforming Mars or building large structures in space, robots are really the only way to do it. Since they can work in conditions humans literally cannot survive in, it means they help us transcend our limitations in a very real way, at least in that context.

Tesla and SpaceX founder Elon Musk, the entrepreneur who wants to send the human race to Mars, also believes that "to avoid becoming redundant in the face of the development of artificial intelligence, humans must merge with machines to enhance our own intellect."[13]

Robot exploration helps improve our knowledge of the outer planets, stars, asteroids, comets (Rosetta); orbiters and landers are sent to remote places even if it takes time for the travel with the present state of our technology.

While you might think that transhumanists only care about technologies that affect their individual bodies or lifespans, the fate of human beings as a species is also a key topic. There are many reasons to care about outer space when it comes to the meaning of being human or what it means to be more than human.

Sending a robot to space is also much cheaper than sending a human. We can send robots to explore space without having to worry so much about their safety. Robots do not need to eat or sleep or go to the bathroom. They can survive in space for many years and can be left out there with no need for a return trip! Robots can do lots of things that humans cannot. Some can withstand harsh conditions, like extreme temperatures, or high levels of radiation. See "Man or robots in space":[14] NASA, for its part, takes a neutral stance ("We need both!"), hoping that the controversy will go away.[15]

So before terraforming Mars for a human presence, it is first necessary to ensure that robots would not be the more realistic solution. This will be discussed in the following sections.

---

[13] See above note 7.

[14] *Robots in Space*, Roger D Launius and Howard E McCurdy, John Hopkins University Press, 2008.

[15] "Humans vs. Robots" Tony Reichhardt, *Airspacemag.com*, June 26, 2008. Read more at: https://www.airspacemag.com/space/humans-vs-robots-180653/#mb6im1fbIaQieaBW.99

2.2. *Next targets*

Moon has been a first and fantastic step in the space conquest. Now, a half century has elapsed since the historical Apollo 11 mission, on July 24 1969, when Eagle landed on the "Sea of Tranquility". Neil Armstrong was the first man to make "the great leap for mankind".

Some years ago I had the opportunity to visit the spacecraft Apollo 11 and a copy of the lunar module. I was surprised that the technology used was not an "up to date" one: old cathodic tubes, mechanical switches, etc… The explanation was that space technology requires a high reliability and the designers often prefer old but time-tested, field-proven components even if less performing. This is still somewhat true nowadays.

Mars is the most remote planet that has already been explored with rovers (Curiosity, Spirit of Opportunity, and others) or any kind of probe. Expectations are formulated to send a human crew there in the near future even if we do know that the travel will be especially difficult and the return to Earth presently virtually impossible. Nevertheless there are already some promising candidates ready for the trip!

Other possibilities are already explored such as Titan, the largest Moon of Saturn, which has a dense atmosphere, lakes of hydrocarbons, ice, etc… Titan resembles a primitive Earth at a much lower temperature. This is far from an Eden but…some have suggested that there could be a kind of prebiotic life.[16]

3. Are There Other Living Species Somewhere in Space?

That is the biggest question still unanswered.

3.1. *Research on the origin of life*

If we humans are not the only intelligent life form in the universe, space is where we will find the others. That remains a delicate point for transhumanists. Why does that matter? One of the ways we can unlock the

---

[16]"Saturn's Moon Titan Prebiotic Laboratory", Jonathan Lunine, *Astrobiology Magazine*, August 11, 2004.

mysteries of the universe, and understand our own nature and place in the universe better, is through learning from intelligent species that could live in our galaxy.

Transhumanists such as Ray Kurzweil, support the SETI[17] organization but they admit that this is a haystack we have just begun to tackle to find the proverbial needle. The Allen radio-telescope array is especially devoted to this particular study of the quest of planets which could accommodate a kind of life. Any "civilization", as ours, generates an electromagnetic activity which can be detected from far away. Our electromagnetic emissions constantly increase and so too our intelligence. So it is hoped that sooner or later a contact could be taken with other developed civilizations.

3.2. *Transformation of man and the no-return travel*

Transhumanists claim that we are on the verge of entering a Type II level civilization which will require inescapable deep changes in both our human nature and our environment.

Only half a century ago, Man had begun to take his first steps into outer space, thus leaving his mother planet. He so got rid of gravity for the first time in his long history and right away he realized that there would be, in the long run, deep implications on his own biological makeup. This would lead to a new appropriate 2.0 man species. Would he reproduce as usual or would he better have to take the opportunity of (cheapest and easier to implement) artificial biological reproduction, a solution especially well designed for the purpose?

Humans are ill-suited to the rigors of space, but augmenting ourselves with technology may create opportunities to explore and colonize worlds beyond our own.

The anthropic principle: How do we account for the remarkable design of the laws and constants of matter and energy in our universe that have allowed for the increasing complexity we see in biological and technology evolution? Freeman Dyson once commented that "the universe in some sense knew we were coming".

---

[17] Search for Extra Terrestrial Intelligence.

This has opened the door for advocates of intelligent design to claim that this is the proof of God's existence that scientists have been asking for. Space does, however, contain all of the frontiers that we know of and all of those we do not yet recognize.

The Earth is a tiny planet in a nondescript corner of a big galaxy, which is nonetheless only one of about two trillion galaxies in our universe. Meanwhile, all of human history and just about everything that has ever been of any direct interest to humans has happened on this one tiny planet.

Space is fascinating and terrifying at the same time and, depending on our emerging path, the future of humanity might lay in the stars. There are many reasons to care about outer space when it comes to the meaning of being human or what it means to be more than human.

Our first stop will most likely be Mars. In this section, the colonization of Mars has a prominent place since we are very close to getting humans (and perhaps even a permanent base) on the red planet's surface.

If we humans are not the only intelligent life forms in the universe, whether space is where we will find the others or the fate of human beings as a species, is also a key topic. There are many reasons to care about outer space when it comes to the meaning of being human or what it means to be more than human.

3.3. Toward artificial explorers? Mind uploading?

After exploring the nearby environment of the Earth and even Moon, ambitions have extended to the very deep space where there is no provision for a homecoming on planet Earth. This means that deep changes are to be expected for the "space settlers" dedicated to Mars or even the more distant Titan orbiting around Saturn. Some have already planned to create dedicated "improved" men to face the harsh conditions of space travel (radiations) and survival in a different environment. Is that expansion of Humanity a God's will or more simply a testimony of Man's insanity? Would Man also have to export the idea of God in his bag and build a church or a shrine on Titan? Whatever are the answers, that expansion will occur soon. This is no longer in the realm of science fiction.

There is a less risky approach which was already largely implemented up to now, that is to send "robots" instead of men! Such robots have to be (and are) increasingly intelligent to make them prepared to face any unpredictable situations (as a man could do). This would imply that robots would have to be taught the notion of danger and threats that they originally lack, if they "want to survive". In any case they should have the first duty to account in real time what is going on in their operations.

This outer space exploration project might sound crazy but nevertheless follows the same instinctive need that led our human ancestors to cross the oceans on fragile boats or cross the deserts without any knowledge of what could lie beyond the horizon. Only the scale has changed! Christopher Colombus left Spain towards the West in order (it was his initial intent) to reach China (Cipango) by a shorter route. That was how he discovered America! So we must not be surprised if our future explorations also lead us to unexpected results!

3.4. Cryonics? Cyborgization?

Mars is the most remote planet that is already explored with rovers (Curiosity, Spirit of Opportunity, and others) or any kind of probe. Expectations are formulated to send there a human crew in a near future even if we do know that the travel will be especially difficult and the return to Earth presently virtually impossible. Nevertheless there are already candidates ready for the trip!

If we humans are not the only intelligent life form in the universe, space is where we will find the others. That remains a delicate point for transhumanists. Why does that matter? One of the ways we can unlock the mysteries of the universe, and understand our own nature and place in the universe better, is through learning from intelligent species that live in our galaxy. They could possibly be less advanced in the evolution run but also, as well, be much more advanced. In any case the meeting would be of the highest interest. This will bring us close to Science Fiction with the deep question of the UFO. This subject is not a fancy even if it could look unrealistic. The evidence is that in every developed country there is a special service (often a little bit secret) devoted to gather the various testimonies they could collect from random and uncertain observations.

4. UFOs: Robots or Aliens?

A wealth of observations of strange and unknowable objects has been reported for a very long time. Some are unquestionably to be considered as unreliable, fantasist, belonging to delusion, or pure invention. However the numerous other observations of "True Believers" were serious, detailed, and justified testimonies that might not be discarded *a priori*. Some people evoke the possibility of super, stealth, secret aircrafts developed by governments (namely the U.S.) which "brand those who saw them as deluded fools or cranks".

Obviously such a subject could not leave indifferent the transhumanists and their Super Technological Singularity.[18]

4.1. *Unexplained phenomena*

These observations could refer to unexplained physical, natural phenomena[19] or to still more unexplained ones related to space "travelers" in outer space. Most of the time, "flying saucers" are pointed out, which could be

---

[18] "UFO and the transhumanists", Dirk Bruere, July 14, 2018. Available at: — https://medium.com/@dirk.bruere/ufos-and-transhumanism-7d12551ff370

[19] I do have myself witnessed such a phenomenon which I am (as an experienced physicist) fully unable to explain.

On a hot summer starry night, I was lying in my bed looking at the deep blue sky through an open window at two in the morning, failing asleep. All a sudden I clearly saw a pale uniformly white ball, the apparent size of a full moon which crossed the sky horizontally at high speed (a matter of two seconds to cross the observation field). No noise, no smoke, no trail, no blinking. A simple calculation supposing the "object" at a distance of 10 km (which is a maximum) gave me a speed of 20,000 km/h and a size in the range of 300 m !

I have not any available explanation to suggest but I am fully certain of what I have seen. That "object" did not resemble anything belonging to our material world (even a lightning in ball). If somebody gets an idea, please, tell me, I would appreciate! What strikes me is the infinitesimal probability for me to have been the lucky spectator of such a show!

a sort of vehicle sheltering a crew of non-human beings. These vehicles would possibly move at incredible speeds without any noise and breaking elementary rules of inertia and gravity. We are in the ET world!

Transhumanists are fond of proposing avatars, either machines or biological entities beyond any human present capabilities.

4.2. Are we animals in a zoo?

The remaining unanswered questions are: if there are visitors from outside (be they "biologic", robots, or a combination of that) why did they never try to show up and contact us? Where, the hell, are they coming from? Would they be afraid of human behavior? Are they much too smart and intelligent or not enough? Or more simply, we don't see them because they have found staying at home far more interesting than zooming around as tourists.

Yet, for a while, we have been looking pretty hard, scanning the galaxy (and outside) for any sign that we are not alone in the universe. But we looked in vain to the heavens and no one really knows why. Would we be alone? That seems a bit difficult to swallow.

From an external point of view, would our humanity only be no more than a matter of curiosity? In such a case would the Earth would look like a kind of zoo where aliens come for fun? Do we in fact live in an alien-created virtual reality?

Then comes the Fermi paradox: "in all this space, and all this time, there should be plenty of advanced alien civilizations — but we haven't heard from any of them. How come?" But, "One of the big problems with our understandings of aliens has to do with Hollywood. Movies and television have led us to think of aliens as green, slimy creatures traveling around in flying saucers."[20]

The transhumanist position for explaining the unexplainable of a future "humanity+" propose that "the merging of the organic with the synthetic is not just an option at the end of *Mass Effect*, but a plotline we are actively choosing with every passing day." Or, as Charlie Huenemann

---

[20] "Why haven't we met aliens yet? Because they've evolved into AI", Zoltan Istvan, *Vice*, March 16, 2016. Available at: — https://www.vice.com/en_us/article/vv7bkb/why-havent-we-met-aliens-yet-because-theyve-evolved-into-ai

said: "Maybe the aliens have checked us out already and decided to put us in galactic time-out; maybe they already walk among us; maybe tomorrow we will indeed make contact; maybe alien governments always decide to cut funding for alien NASA programs; maybe in fact we live in an alien-created virtual reality". As proposed by Nick Boström there could be chances that we are (or intended to become) "sims" living in a simulation![21]

Why do transhumanists care about the outer space and aliens when it comes to the meaning of being human or may be more than human? They said that, one day we may find new places to call home among the stars. Our spaceship, the Earth, won't be around forever,[22] so, maybe, we will have to "negotiate" with aliens if we plan to invade their domain!

As a matter of fact, as Shakespeare said in Ophelia: "we know what we are, but know not what we may be. God be at your table!"

---

[21] "The Fermi paradox, mass effect, and Transhumanism", Charlie Huenemann, *3 Quarks Daily*, April 13, 2015. Available at: — https://www.3quarksdaily.com/3quarksdaily/2015/04/the-fermi-paradox-mass-effect-and-transhumanism.html

[22] "About space, transhumanism and extraterrestrial life", *Human Paragon*. Available at: https://humanparagon.com/space/

Conclusion

Would this Conclusion be a balance-sheet or a prediction of the future? Nobody knows where we are going to, but we certainly are going somewhere very different from what we know thus far! The acceleration of our fate is there, we can take it for sure.

The Transhumanism "philosophy" has appeared as an extrapolation of the consequences of our extending knowledge and knowhow. What to conclude about the future? Where are we heading to (together?)? Everything's possible, including the worst, but what will be, will be, as the song says.

We do are now in the 2.0 world of this 21st century. The laws of nature fade out and allow human decisions to take over. The evolution process is still active but it has got a bit frenzied and overruled by technology.

Transhumanism is neither a religion, nor a sect. It is only an intellectual movement of people who are interested in the amazing advances of the 2.0 sciences and technologies. They expect that extrapolations could be made to imagine a possible close future.

Scientists are a main source of information but they do not contribute directly to the transhumanism thinking and there is not any famous scientist involved in the brain trust. The contributors are mainly dedicated philosophers such as Ray Kurzweil, Nick Boström, David Pearce, Hans Moravec, Marvin Minsky, and many others.

Their many concerns are focused on the future of Man as a living species. His deep nature is now endangered by the new perspectives opened by genetics, stem cells tissue reconstruction, brain exploration, or AI. Is man to become a new creature? The aim is to overcome the limits.

All of that no longer makes place for the traditional idea of God and its creation: Nature. No more Heaven is expected, no Hell to fear! Man is left faced with himself. Child mortality has definitively disappeared and natural selection vanished; we are on the verge of creating life from scratch and directly challenge God!

Some predictions can already be guessed as the extension of the life span; such a shift is already noticeable[1] in the statistics but R Kurzweil, for his own part, anticipates a life expectancy in the range of 150 years for soon. Also rejuvenation, ageing reversal or artificial creation of life are terminologies often found in the transhumanist's discourse.

There is at the same time a powerful evocation of the present advances in robotics and AI which makes thinkable a mixing of Man with machines leading to the creation of Cyborgs or, even worse, a blunt transfer of mind in a computer. That is the universe evoked by the transhumanist philosophers. Are they right, would we have the ways and the means to continue this way?

Anyway, there are also anticipated limits on the ground as well as in space with the requirement of enough requisite material resources and energy.

Another important point often evoked: the conquest of the deep space could, as imagined by some, become a basic necessity if humanity were to leave the Earth (for any dramatic reason) and seek refuge elsewhere.

Does all of that belong to a realistic future? Only God knows!

---

[1] Fillard, *Longevity*.

Printed in the United States
By Bookmasters